The Dynamics of Social Capital in Romania's IT&C Sector

Diana Ivana · Diana Pitic · Tudor Irimiaș ·
Daniel Metz · Sorin Dan · Diana Ghenie

The Dynamics of Social Capital in Romania's IT&C Sector

Reshaping the Future of Work

Diana Ivana
Faculty of Economics and Business Administration
Babeş-Bolyai University
Cluj-Napoca, Romania

Diana Pitic
Faculty of Economics and Business Administration
Babeş-Bolyai University
Cluj-Napoca, Romania

Tudor Irimiaş
Faculty of Economics and Business Administration
Babeş-Bolyai University
Cluj-Napoca, Romania

Daniel Metz
Faculty of Law and Social Sciences
1 Decembrie 1918 University of Alba Iulia
Alba Iulia, Romania

Sorin Dan
School of Management
University of Vaasa
Vaasa, Finland

Diana Ghenie
Faculty of Economics and Business Administration
Babeş-Bolyai University
Cluj-Napoca, Romania

ISBN 978-3-032-01873-1   ISBN 978-3-032-01874-8 (eBook)
https://doi.org/10.1007/978-3-032-01874-8

© The Editor(s) (if applicable) and The Author(s), under exclusive license to Springer Nature Switzerland AG 2025

This work is subject to copyright. All rights are solely and exclusively licensed by the Publisher, whether the whole or part of the material is concerned, specifically the rights of translation, reprinting, reuse of illustrations, recitation, broadcasting, reproduction on microfilms or in any other physical way, and transmission or information storage and retrieval, electronic adaptation, computer software, or by similar or dissimilar methodology now known or hereafter developed.
The use of general descriptive names, registered names, trademarks, service marks, etc. in this publication does not imply, even in the absence of a specific statement, that such names are exempt from the relevant protective laws and regulations and therefore free for general use.
The publisher, the authors and the editors are safe to assume that the advice and information in this book are believed to be true and accurate at the date of publication. Neither the publisher nor the authors or the editors give a warranty, expressed or implied, with respect to the material contained herein or for any errors or omissions that may have been made. The publisher remains neutral with regard to jurisdictional claims in published maps and institutional affiliations.

Cover illustration: © Melisa Hasan

This Palgrave Macmillan imprint is published by the registered company Springer Nature Switzerland AG
The registered company address is: Gewerbestrasse 11, 6330 Cham, Switzerland

If disposing of this product, please recycle the paper.

Preface

This book, *The Dynamics of Social Capital in Romania's IT&C Sector: Reshaping the Future of Work*, explores the profound transformations that have taken place in the dynamics of social capital in the IT&C sector in the context of the accelerated changes brought about by the COVID-19 pandemic. This period of global crisis has forced companies to rethink traditional ways of working and rapidly develop innovative models of communication and relationship building, adapted to the new realities. The hybrid work model has emerged as the dominant preference among employees and employers alike, bringing flexibility and efficiency. However, our research shows that the need for direct human connection remains strong. People still want to interact face to face, collaborate authentically and feel part of a vibrant professional community.

The book is the result of a collaboration between the Faculty of Economics and Business Administration at the Babeș-Bolyai University, NTT DATA Romania and the School of Management of the University of Vaasa, Finland. We would like to express our sincere gratitude to the management of our institutions for their support. The partnership between academia and practice provided the ideal context for an applied and relevant analysis with direct implications for organisational management.

We believe that this research makes a significant contribution to understanding how social capital is evolving in the post-pandemic era and highlights its importance in shaping the future of work. We hope that this book will be a source of inspiration for researchers, practitioners, leaders and decision-makers in the IT&C sector.

Cluj-Napoca, Romania Diana Ivana
Alba Iulia, Romania Diana Pitic
Vaasa, Finland Tudor Irimiaș
 Daniel Metz
 Sorin Dan
 Diana Ghenie

Acknowledgements We would like to express our special thanks to the management of the Faculty of Economics and Business Administration at the Babeș-Bolyai University, the University of Vaasa and NTT DATA Romania. We are also grateful to team members at NTT DATA Romania for their constant support and active involvement in this project. We particularly appreciate the contribution of the staff who facilitated the data collection process, providing essential logistical and operational support for the smooth running of the research. We would also like to thank all the respondents who took the time to answer the questionnaires and interviews. Without their openness and availability, this work would have not been possible.

Competing Interests The authors Dr. Diana Ivana, Dr. Diana Pitic, Dr. Tudor Irimiaș. Dr. Daniel Metz, Dr. Sorin Dan and Drd. Diana Ghenie declare none.

Dr. Diana Ivana is currently working full-time in the higher education sector while also having a part-time collaboration agreement with the company under study.

At the time of the study, Dr. Daniel Metz served as chairman of the company's board of directors and is currently engaged in full-time work in higher education.

Ethics Approvals This research project has received the research ethics approval granted by the Scientific Council of the Babeș-Bolyai University of Cluj-Napoca, No. 2631 /03.03.2023.

Contents

1 Introduction—Navigating the Evolving IT&C Landscape   1
   1.1 *The Concept of OSC and its Relevance to the IT&C Sector. The Impact of Remote and Hybrid Work on Organisational Dynamics*   1
   1.2 *Literature Review on OSC and Remote Work*   4
   1.3 *Introduction to the Case Study and the Organisational Setting*   13
   References   16

2 Structural Elements of Organisational Social Capital   21
   2.1 *Research Design and Methods*   21
   2.2 *Key Findings*   27
      2.2.1 *Macrolevel Structural Elements of OSC*   27
      2.2.2 *Microlevel Structural Elements of OSC*   29
   References   34

3 Organisational Social Capital Influencing Factors   37
   3.1 *Influencing Factor Number 1: Interaction*   38
      3.1.1 *Forms of Interaction*   39
      3.1.2 *Benefits and Quality of In-person Interaction*   40
      3.1.3 *Input from Clients, Managers and Colleagues*   41
   3.2 *Influencing Factor Number 2: Interdependence*   42
      3.2.1 *Functional Interdependence*   42

  3.2.2 Relational Interdependence as a Mechanism
     to Address Turnover and Improve Retention. 43
  3.2.3 Pooled Interdependence 45
  3.2.4 Sequential Interdependence 46
  3.2.5 Reciprocal Interdependence 46
  3.2.6 Team's Autonomy Degree 47
 3.3 Influencing Factor Number 3: Stability
   (Organisational (in)Stability and (Dis)Continuity) 48
  3.3.1 (In)stability and (Dis)continuity
     in Functional/Departmental Teams 51
  3.3.2 (In)stability and (Dis)continuity in Social
     and People Structures Overall 53
  3.3.3 Client Perceptions About Company's
     (In)stability and (Dis)continuity
     and the Influence of the Labour Market 54
 3.4 Influencing Factor Number 4: Closure 55
  3.4.1 Sense of Belonging 55
  3.4.2 Self-identification as an Employee 56
  3.4.3 Self-differentiation from Other Employees
     in Similar Companies 56

**4 Navigating the Future: Insights and Adaptations
 in Organisational Landscape 59**
 4.1 Future Work Scenarios 60
 4.2 Future Possibilities 65
 4.3 Managerial Recommendations 71
 References 76

**5 Concluding Reflections on the Implications of Social
 Capital for the Future of Work 79**
 References 83

Appendix 1 Interview Question Matrix 85

About the Authors

Diana Ivana (PhD, Babeş-Bolyai University) is a Lecturer at Babeş-Bolyai University and an HR Manager in the IT&C sector. Her expertise encompasses talent management and entrepreneurship, with a particular emphasis on the technology and communications fields. Her research and teaching are informed by her practical experience in aligning HR strategies with the evolving needs of the industry. She has authored over 15 academic publications, including *Digital Talent Management*, published by Palgrave Macmillan, which offers a unique perspective bridging academic theory and real-world practice.

Diana Pitic PhD is an Associate Professor at the Babeş-Bolyai University, Faculty of Economics and Business Administration. Her teaching and research activities enclose various management topics such as organisational excellence, governance and stakeholder management. Within her works, we can mark books and book chapters, journal articles and conference papers, as well as membership within several research projects, activities that validate her proficiency and management-related expertise.

Tudor Irimiaş PhD in Engineering and Management, is a Lecturer at the Babeş-Bolyai University, Faculty of Economics and Business Administration, the German Study Line. Tudor is teaching various management and subjects related to informatics and is passionate about exploring how he can increase students' engagement in the pedagogical process and enrich their learning experiences through business simulation games. Consequently, his research endeavours primarily deal with the outcomes of simulation games in higher education, but he also keeps a special place in his heart for organisational studies in multicultural contexts and employees' perspectives about organisational and individual change.

Daniel Metz (PhD, Babes-Bolyai University) is a University Professor and Vice-Rector at "1 Decembrie 1918" University of Alba Iulia. With over 20 years of experience as the CEO of one of the largest IT companies in Romania, he has played a key role in developing the country's tech industry. His academic contributions are equally notable, with numerous publications in the field of management and a strong focus on leadership and innovation. Throughout his career, Mr. Daniel Metz has been involved in various educational and research initiatives, making significant contributions to both the academic and business sectors.

Sorin Dan (PhD in Social Sciences, KU Leuven, Belgium) is an Assistant Professor in Public Management at the University of Vaasa School of Management, Vaasa, Finland. His areas of expertise include public sector reforms and digital transformation. He has offered consultancy services to the OECD and the European Commission and has authored over 30 scholarly publications, including *Digital Talent Management: Insights from the Information Technology and Communication Industry* (2021) and *The Coordination of European Public Hospital Systems: Interests, Cultures and Resistance* (2017), published by Palgrave Macmillan.

Diana Ștefania Ghenie (PhD student, Babeș-Bolyai University) is a Graduate of the International Management Master's programme in German within the Faculty of Economics and Business Administration, Babeș-Bolyai University of Cluj-Napoca, Romania. She is also a PhD student in the field of Business Information Systems at the Faculty of Economics and Business Administration, Babeș-Bolyai University of Cluj-Napoca, Romania.

List of Figures

Fig. 1.1 Remote work representation (*Source* Pixabay)   3
Fig. 1.2 Research framework   15

List of Tables

Table 2.1 Demographic dataset   24
Table 4.1 Effects of the "remote" work model   72

CHAPTER 1

Introduction—Navigating the Evolving IT&C Landscape

Abstract This chapter lays the foundation for the research by contextualising the significance of social capital in the IT&C sector. It presents the concept of social capital and explores how the latter can improve organisational performance and the trend towards telecommuting. It particularly examines how the COVID-19 pandemic hastened changes in corporate culture, communication and teamwork in the IT&C sector. This chapter also includes a brief review of the literature and the introduction to case study and organisational setting.

Keywords Organisational social capital · IT&C sector · Post COVID-19 context · Hybrid organisations

1.1 The Concept of OSC and its Relevance to the IT&C Sector. The Impact of Remote and Hybrid Work on Organisational Dynamics

In the current unpredictable environment, companies must devise ongoing solutions to address global competitiveness and swiftly changing client demands. One of the greatest challenges in the contemporary era in which companies must face different challenges regarding productivity and sustainability at the workplace is the development of human resources and social capital which has been acknowledged as a novel instrument for enhancing organisational performance as well as the importance of social interactions and relationships at individual, group and organisational levels (Hafermalz & Riemer, 2020; Hassard & Morris, 2024; Lenz et al., 2023).

The IT&C sector was selected for this study for two key reasons: first, because it is the industry most responsive to pandemic-driven changes, offering remote work opportunities, and second, due to its significant role in Romania's economy, contributing substantially to national income, exports and foreign investment. The sector's strong technological culture, deeply rooted in Romania's educational system, especially in IT, positions it as a potential driver of economic prosperity (Vaduva & Neagoie, 2016). Therefore, the skilled workforce and the employment growth provide the IT&C sector in Romania a boost to become a key factor in the country's continuous economic growth (Dan et al., 2021). Furthermore, the IT&C sector has suffered the most from the COVID-19 pandemic, especially in relation to the rising telework and work-from-home trend. The European Commission released research which analyses the level of telework in the EU before and after the crisis, considering the impact on diverse regions, sectors and professions. Clear disparities in telework emerged among EU member states, industries and professions following the outbreak of the pandemic. There is evidence that the IT&C and knowledge-intensive sectors and sectors with high-skilled workers had better telework preparedness (European Union, 2020).

Novel survival challenges for enterprises have emerged, which forced companies to respond promptly and adapt their operations to sustain business continuity, along with effectively and efficiently overseeing remote work and employee turnover (Fig. 1.1). The literature also highlights a tendency among leaders to delegate more and exercise less control (Ajith et al., 2024). Alongside companies, employees also had to adapt, learn and develop new sets of skills (Rozkwitalska-Welenc, 2024).

Research on organisational social capital (OSC) has investigated the impact of four primary elements influencing OSC development: stability, interaction, interdependence and closure (Nahapiet & Ghoshal, 1998). Still, employee turnover constitutes an important expense for companies, which can contribute to the change in OSC. Organisations incur expenses associated with hiring and training of new employees to replace those who left the company. There are also costs associated with turnover, such as

Fig. 1.1 Remote work representation (*Source* Pixabay)

the loss of skills, networks and social capital resulting from individuals leaving the companies (Kellogg, 2021).

Future workspaces had to be increasingly flexible, decentralised and centred on individuals to attract and retain top talent, while fostering energy and creativity in both remote and in-person settings. For numerous companies, the early stages of the epidemic and the shift to remote work resulted in greater production output (Bird, 2021).

Despite the unpredictability and instability of the global crisis, many organisations benefited from a solid basis of social capital cultivated through prior long-term collaboration and face-to-face interactions. Pre-existing social capital enabled a seamless transition to working remotely while maintaining an awareness of the broader corporate context.

Moreover, alongside expertise and experience, it was essential to include employees' capacity to cultivate social networks that foster diverse communication and trust frameworks, wherein organisational social capital is established, thereby enhancing value creation (Carmona-Lavado, Cuevas-Rodríguez & Cabello-Medina, 2010).

Based on discussions with the business community, we concluded that the post-pandemic work-from-home model has enabled employees in the IT&C sector to work for any employer, regardless of their location. This flexibility allowed many employees to consider and accept attractive offers they might have previously declined due to relocation requirements. Consequently, the industry experienced a significant wave of departures, and HR specialists handling off-boarding processes noted that the primary reason cited by many was a diminishing sense of connection to the organisational culture due to remote work.

This research was therefore initiated out of a desire to rebuild these connections, even within a hybrid environment. The research first establishes a theoretical framework for building and strengthening organisational social capital specifically tailored for the information technology and communications (IT&C) sector. This framework is grounded in the pioneering works of Leana and Van Buren (1999) and Nahapiet and Ghoshal (1998) and it seeks to provide insights into how organisational dynamics within this industry are influenced by the increasing prevalence of remote and hybrid work environments.

1.2 Literature Review on OSC and Remote Work

The concept of social capital (SC) in businesses is relatively new, having been in the spotlight since Nahapiet and Ghoshal's article (1998) gave impetus to the issue in the literature. According to Nahapiet and Ghoshal (1998), social capital fosters the development of intellectual capital, and organisations are supportive of building up social capital. The organisational social capital (OSC) term was later introduced by Leana and Van Buren (1999), describing OSC as a "resource reflecting the character of social relations within the organisation". Since then, various conceptualisations have emerged; however, its nature, structural elements and boundaries remain subjects of debate. A phenomenon similar to SC has been observed: there is a "genotype" of SC, with many different "phenotypes" (definitions and applications) that continue to evolve and diversify over time (Adam & Rončević, 2003).

Furthermore, social capital theory has been used to analyse knowledge sharing within a company (van Bakel & Horak, 2024). Due to its connection to information sharing and ability to facilitate cross-border coordination and cooperation, social capital is essential to the success of multinational corporations (van Bakel & Horak, 2024).

There have been several calls in the recent literature on the need to incorporate contextual factors in OSC studies (Erdreich, 2024; Sanchez-Famoso et al., 2019). OSC is a key concept in organisation theory that manifests relationally through social ties, personal interaction and functional interdependence at work (Ben Hador, 2017). We view OSC as an attribute of organisations, defined as "a resource reflecting the character of social relations within the organisation, realised through members' levels of collective goal orientation and shared trust, which create value by facilitating collective social action" (Leana & van Buren, 1999, 538).

The study by Roman and Smida (2015) was also considered, as it underscores the peculiarities of OSC in multinational companies within the IT&C sector. The findings of this research indicate the high market demands, the complexity of the products and services offered, long-term projects that such organisations must undertake daily, interdisciplinarity and the need for teamwork to create an environment in which OSC becomes a critical resource. At the same time, research about the impact of the COVID-19 pandemic on OSC in the IT&C sector brings to the fore the idea that companies have a drawing preference to offer the possibility of work from home or work from anywhere (Rupic, 2024).

It is worth mentioning that the IT&C sector has been significantly impacted by the COVID-19 pandemic. While navigating the pandemic itself was challenging, managing its aftermath remains an ongoing struggle. There are very few studies in the specialised literature on the topic of OSC in IT&C companies, especially considering that the virtualisation of activities became more prominent in this sector after the pandemic. Moreover, in Romania, IT companies have undergone significant changes in their social capital due to both the pandemic and the business model used, with most of them being acquired by large companies, requiring their values to be aligned with those of the larger companies.

Over the last years, multiple changes challenged the shape of future organisations, emerging from multiple facets of both social and economic goals to be pursued at the same time. Scholars and practitioners relied on current existing knowledge and experiences in establishing possible future configurations of work arrangements, work structures, new ways of recruiting, onboarding while managing remotely. Existing experiences can be found in the literature that addressed stakeholder theory (Cots, 2011; Sen & Cowley, 2012) and change management, thus incorporating reactive and proactive leading possibilities, but also responses to crisis situations and the role of human resources in a broader sense, human capital and social capital in a narrower sense. Still, multiple open-ended questions derive from the need for consensus regarding future work arrangements, both a confrontation and mitigation between employees and employers.

The broader theoretical framework of stakeholder theory also plays a significant role in understanding this subject (Freeman et al., 2004), where long-term value should be achieved for all stakeholders, whereas the initial shareholder theory pursues reaching financial goals for companies' ownership. Main prerequisites require that organisations should identify and consider both internal and external stakeholders, understand and integrate their requirements and develop such a setting that enables surpassing the focus on shareholders and enhancing the value creation of organisations for them to have both long-term success while being sustainable (Mahajan et al., 2023). In pursuing such an approach, managers must be fluent in expressing which are the goals of the company and the sense of the shared value they create, thus making clear what convenes stakeholders and what kind of relationships are about to be built and therefore the essence of the stakeholder theory is revealed: companies' financial rewards in form of profits are merely the result of human resources that work together for common goals and thus, managers must grow such relationships that become meaningful, inspiring and empower employees in delivering the values undertaken by the company (Freeman et al., 2004).

Further answers that complement open-ended questions regarding the (re)shaping of organisations might be found in the theory addressing hybrid organisations, which merge economic and social goals, thus embracing profitability and improving the social environment. In the same line of thought, such organisations help bridging both social and environmental challenges and provide clients with social value (unlike traditional organisations) (Cantin et al., 2021), therefore creating their own competitive advantage, enhancing employee engagement, improving performance and sharing knowledge (Bhatti et al., 2020). Nonetheless, for such value to be delivered, an innovative approach towards the allocation of resources arises, hence both the economic and social values are pursued to be reached at the same time. Therefore, further conflicts are likely to arise, potentially leading stakeholders, employees and business partners to dissent, making it difficult for them to effectively work towards shared goals while also pursuing their individual objectives. One way to address these situations is by establishing "negotiation spaces" where all parties can openly share perspectives and collaborate on strategies to achieve both economic and social objectives (Battilana et al., 2015). For such spaces to be effective, intense, active social interaction is necessary, as well as formal structures that support their initiation and development (Cantin et al., 2021).

The need for consensus between own, personal goals and the ones of the organisation is evident, and the remaining issue is how to build up such relationships that enable bonding, shared identity, shared ideas and enhance trust, resulting in reciprocal exchanges of resources (Erdreich, 2024), marked by elements of organisational culture that regulate norms, rules, relationships and obligations which, in turn, have a significant impact on the outcome of organisational performance (Bhatti et al., 2020). It is therefore essential to establish connections within the organisation with a hybrid role to facilitate the sharing and exchange of information and ideas and to achieve consensus among the groups representing divergent interests (Amonarriz et al., 2019).

In this context, social capital, as a component of intellectual capital (Bhatti et al., 2020), would play a crucial role in building up networks between the parties involved (Cantin et al., 2021), much like a woven structure, fostering the exchange of ideas and information and thus cannot exist independently. Instead, it is rooted and shaped by the organisation's members, who embed both tangible and intangible resources that can be activated and applied in daily practice (Adler and Kwon, 2002; Erdreich, 2024). Being perceived as an organisational attribute, the Organisational Social Capital (OSC) is defined, as already mentioned, as "a resource reflecting the character of social relations within the organisation, realised through members' levels of collective goal orientation and shared trust, which create value by facilitating collective social action" (Leana & Van Buren 1999, 538). Also, it is important to mention that social capital has several dimensions, such as structural, cognitive and relational (Nahapiet & Ghoshal, 1998), whereas the research focus is given by the relational social capital. Interestingly, both intellectual capital and social capital require ongoing maintenance, not because they depreciate in the traditional sense, but because they must be continuously developed and reinforced (Adler & Kwon, 2002).

Regarding both enablers and results of social capital, scholars distinguish between bonding capital and bridging capital (Adler & Kwon, 2002; Erdreich, 2024); whereas the former focuses on trust between people and strength of relations, the latter highlights the overlapping connections between people that belong to different social networks. Indeed, significant connections can unite individuals who vary in socially pertinent aspects which help in bridging social capital (Cantin et al., 2021). These bridges are anticipated to be formalised. Secondly, the greater the degree of interconnectedness of hybrid companies, the higher their likelihood of maintaining their survival (Hasenfeld & Gidron, 2005), as this enhances their capacity to mobilise members and secure support.

Thus, social capital contributes to reaching long-term effects, which are relevant from a social and economic perspective. Although social capital is less liquid than economic capital, it can be seen as a complementary resource for an individual or organisation, as it is able to reduce transaction costs, thus contributing towards improving the economic efficiency (Adler & Kwon, 2002). Nevertheless, if and how social capital is important to an organisation, it should be made visible through all formal and informal channels (Cantin et al., 2021) through which information and exchange of knowledge flow easily. Enabling social relationships in an organisation would not only lead to better collaboration among employees but might also help employees in better understanding the organisation's goals, values, norms and adhering thereto. Intense networking and continuous routines facilitate a deeper awareness of the organisation's objectives and reciprocal interdependencies among its participants (Battilana et al., 2015). Identifying constructs of Organisational Social Capital, assessing the degree of exchange and of consensus and (dis)functioning bonding initiatives or activities would therefore require any organisation's attention.

Given the existing literature evidence and its relevance for the IT&C sector, this research offers a deep understanding of the structural elements and influencing factors of OSC. Therefore, in respect of OSC's identified structural elements, within this work, we will address the following elements (Leana & Van Buren, 1999):

Macro and mesolevel structural elements of OSC:

- *Shared identity*: we share the idea of working for the same company and we identify with the company.
- *Collective action*: we work together for common goals.
- Microlevel structural elements of OSC:
- *Associability*: we focus on collective instead of individual goals.
- *Trust*: the organisation and colleagues are trustworthy.

- *Fragile trust*: based on rational calculation of risks and rewards, e.g. as in a transaction, occasional, short-term.
- *Resilient trust*: based on the belief in the moral integrity of colleagues and the organisation, reflecting repeated interactions over a longer period.
- *Dyadic trust*: between two parties who have direct knowledge of each other.
- *Generalised trust:* based not on direct knowledge but on affiliation, reputation, norms and behaviours in the overall organisation.

Further, scholars have examined the influence of four main factors that affect the creation of OSC, namely stability, interaction, interdependence and closure (Nahapiet & Ghoshal, 1998).

- *Stability/continuity* influences OSC over time as social capital provides continuity, structure, reference points and a shared identity within an organisation. As social structures, organisations rely on stability and continuity to carry on their mission. Social capital is a form of "accumulated history, reflecting investments in social relations and social organisation through time" (Nahapiet & Ghoshal, 1998, 257). The emphasis in this research is on stability in personnel (social structures), which is important because social capital accumulates over time and is influenced by changes in personnel and social structures; stability "increases the clarity and visibility of mutual obligations, as well as the development of trust and norms of cooperation" (Nahapiet & Ghoshal, 1998, 76).
- *Interaction* affects social relations, which depend on the ability of stakeholders to interact with and relate to one another for shared meaning and goals. Organisations are characterised by multiple forms of communication and interaction, many of which are increasingly carried out at a distance and mediated by technology and virtualisation. Frequent interaction contributes to OSC whereas a lack of interaction deteriorates it. However, there is a need to understand how different forms of interaction affect OSC, e.g. how hybrid work affects interaction and ultimately OSC.
- *Interdependence* fosters social capital to the extent that organisational actors depend on each other for the attainment of their goals. Conversely, social capital tends to erode if work is being carried out

independently, without the need for support (Nahapiet & Ghoshal, 1998). As opposed to independent work, interdependence is known to increase OSC due to a mutual need for support and interaction; higher levels of social capital are developed in organisational settings with substantial mutual interdependence.
- *Closure* refers to the ability of organisations to develop a sense of community, belonging and identity that distinguishes members from non-members. A too volatile and fluid social structure characterised by openness, rather than closure, tends to affect social capital to the extent that such structures have challenges to develop common norms, a shared identity and mutual trust (Nahapiet & Ghoshal, 1998). The "existence of a sufficient level of ties between members such that adherence to norms is highly likely" (Arregle et al., 2007); the existence of dense social network boundaries that distinguish between members ("us") from non-members ("them"); it facilitates bonding and the development of trust, norms, identity and belonging. Ruiz-Ortaga et al. (2017) have found a positive link between closure and entrepreneurial orientation, which develops through dynamic capabilities, whereas entrepreneurial intention is described by these authors rather in a broader sense and marked as important when developing and crafting solutions to the benefit of the client, adapting to market and other external constraints and responding to future challenges.

Regarding macro and mesolevel structural elements, shared identity seemed to foster better communication among members of the same group (Greenaway et al., 2014), lead to lesser stress and enhance members' well-being (Van Dick et al., 2018). Collective action refers to both individual and collective actors that reach a higher level of social capital through investing and developing their relations and thus having access to information, fostering a so-called collective good (Adler & Kwon, 2002).

Resilient and generalised trust within an organisation is a good indication of strong OSC, unlike systems characterised by fragile and dyadic trust. Trust is widely regarded as essential for modern teams to operate effectively, especially when using virtual tools, and is therefore a defining feature of the hybrid workplace (Feitosa et al., 2020). Navigating the aftermaths of the pandemic, Ajith et al. (2024) found out that trust emerged as an important factor along with digital transformation, hybrid work and resilience. Moreover, shared identity, collective action and associability characterise organisations with strong OSC. Villacé-Molinero et al. (2024) also echo the idea that associability and trust must be viewed as main pillars of OSC, hence they have an important influence on talent retention.

Analytically, we distinguish between stability and closure and interaction and interdependence. Changes in these factors are expected to influence the formation and development of social capital over time (Arregle et al., 2007). Social capital pertains to the collective orientation of personnel towards organisational objectives, together with the mutual trust and connections among them. The emphasis is on the interrelations among employees within the same group, rather than on individual resources, encompassing the organisation as an entire entity.

These resulting relationships integrate abilities, knowledge and personality traits in a distinctive manner, improving the organisation's competitiveness (Dess & Shaw, 2001). The turnover rate within a group or organisation may compromise the social capital, adversely affecting overall organisational effectiveness and performance (Hausknecht & Trevor, 2011).

The cohesion and strengths of relationships among employees within the same group should emphasise collaboration, sharing of knowledge and professional networking, thereby improving the value of this social capital, while simultaneously leading to the adverse effects of potential collective turnover (Dess & Shaw, 2001).

However, the formation and development of social capital is linked to markets and industries' (re)evolutions, observers noting that in case of financial constraints, former social priorities are replaced by economic efficiency. Thus, in crisis situations, resources are shifted towards reaching or maintaining economic goals, resulting in workers' rejection towards change and a feeling of abandonment regarding social aspects (Cantin et al., 2021). Therefore, when organisations with hybrid objectives encounter severe market conditions, it may result in diminished economic productivity and compromised social efficiency (Battilana et al., 2015), undermining the socio-economic balance of their objectives, and interfering with the advancement of social capital. In the event of a monetary crisis that generates tension, the motivation to enhance efficiency results in austerity measures and raises employees' anxiety (Cervero-Liceras et al.,

2015). In both scenarios, the absence or deficit of established protocols fosters the polarisation of connections, complicating the reaching of consensus among different goals.

Such crisis has been marked by the COVID-19 pandemic (Rupcic, 2024), where one can notice specific aftermaths for the IT&C sector: the preference and the expectancy for companies to offer work-from-home or work-from-anywhere options as a compulsory benefit within a recruiting package. During the pandemic, companies made significant efforts in ensuring this desired outcome, which in turn generated challenges such as lack of identification with the company goals, values and norms, grounded on social isolation. Embedding social capital in such circumstances is a double-edged sword: on the one hand essential for reducing isolation, successful onboarding of newcomers, bonding capital, and on the other hand difficult to achieve when employees prefer a work-from-home status quo. Perez Fernandez et al. (2024) aimed to study whether online social capital and offline social capital have any influence on entrepreneurship intentions and thus found out that online social capital has lesser influence on social norms in comparison with offline social capital. This thus raises important question marks on whether, how and if social capital in an online setting can still foster building up and familiarity with norms, rules and relationships within companies.

Given the significant insights emerged from literature and still ongoing post-pandemic effects, dealing with *the characteristics of social capital in a hybrid work setting* (as our main research direction), two important research questions arise:

Rq1: What are the peculiarities of OSC creation in the IT&C sector?

Rq2: What novel influencing factors of OSC are emerging in the mindset of IT&C professionals?

We rely on investigating possible answers to this question by drawing up a case study encompassing interviews with employees of a company within the IT&C sector after the pandemic and investigating how social capital is perceived in each of its constructs; therefore, social capital is or should be of great importance for organisations that build up their business model relying on social networks (Bhatti et al., 2020), the IT&C sector being one such example. Also, the notion of social capital has been so far mainly studied within SMEs, whereas several results of this category cannot be scaled to larger companies (Cots, 2011; Sen & Cowley, 2012), an additional reason to perform a study within a larger company. In the later chapters of this work, we grasp interviewees' opinions on future work scenarios, future possibilities and new ways that foster social capital.

Such an approach is relevant given the struggles of organisations in juggling multiple goals at the same time, of a somewhat divergent, economic and social nature. Thus, following this roadmap and its results, scholars and practitioners might have an insight as to how and what should or could be an appropriate work setting that continues in building up OSC, therefore enabling the creation of value for both shareholders and stakeholders involved.

1.3 Introduction to the Case Study and the Organisational Setting

How did we set the scene for the research? After the pandemic, the recruitment, motivation and retention process of employees went through vast transformations within the IT&C sector with turnover rates reaching almost 20%. In the case of the analysed company, 25 years in the market: the turnover rate doubled after 2019, when 80% of departures were justified by the belief that "the company is not the same as it was".

To learn the underlying causes, the company teamed up with a university to do deep dive research. This study started with an examination of: (1) the organisation's history, (2) changes in the values articulated in the work as compared to the values shared by the organisation and (3) the effects of virtualisation on employee networking, including employee interactions and connection to the work environment and client relationships. The research first included 8 meetings (each 2 hours long) with the CEO and two HR heads, as well as 20 interviews (1 hour long), 10 with employees who had been with the company since 2000 and 10 with employees who joined the company in the last 5–7 years—to identify both foundational and newly emerging elements of the company's organisational culture. Based on these insights, the company developed the *People Experience Manager* (PEM) initiative to strengthen employee identification with the organisation and reduce turnover.

Following the strategic direction of the organisation, the role of People Experience Manager was summarised by the phrase "Lo♥e your people", which reflects the essence of all initiatives in the company. In this context, a People Experience Framework was developed. Through this initiative in the HR/People area, the company set out to redefine the experience of being part of the organisation, emphasising the quality of organisational life, as perceived by each individual employee. The interaction between colleagues was rethought in a participatory way, using tools and methods to maintain connection. All teams carried out their work guided by values such as respect, empathy and honesty, using validated methodologies such as Design Thinking and Rapid Results, with the aim of building a new framework for the employee experience within the company. People Experience Manager (PEM) had four priority directions: diversity and mutual respect, (re)defining the role of manager, informal activities that connect and create bonds between people and (re)designing a meaningful work environment within the company.

Consequently, we undertook 33 in-depth, semi-structured interviews between February–March 2023, with professionals, all part of the PEM initiative. Employees participating in the programme were interviewed regarding the effectiveness of the programme to understand the impact of networking processes on the organisation's culture, mainly given by the changes in networking during the last two years. The interviews were conducted with 17 women and 16 men, 28 to 58 years old, with an average seniority of about six years. Regarding their job responsibilities, 15 stated that employee management falls within their duties whereas 18 do not have an employee management role. All interviewees have at least a university degree: 12 hold a bachelor's degree, 17 a master's degree and four a doctorate.

The study's data collection was a complex process, addressing a real need for the company to adapt its organisational culture to post-pandemic realities. After being anonymised, the interview transcripts were loaded into MAXQDA 2022 for additional analysis. Following the recommendations of Mayring (2002), Braun and Clarke (2006), and Naeem et al. (2023), the authors who carried out the interviews conducted a qualitative thematic analysis with the aim to identify the organisational and environmental elements that support the formation and growth of OSC.

The book's structure includes the following parts that are covered in five chapters: OSC structural elements (Chapter 2), OSC influencing factors (Chapter 3) and the future of OSC (Chapter 4). Equally, the project's main findings are summarised in the last chapter (5), along with their implications for the IT&C industry (Fig. 1.2).

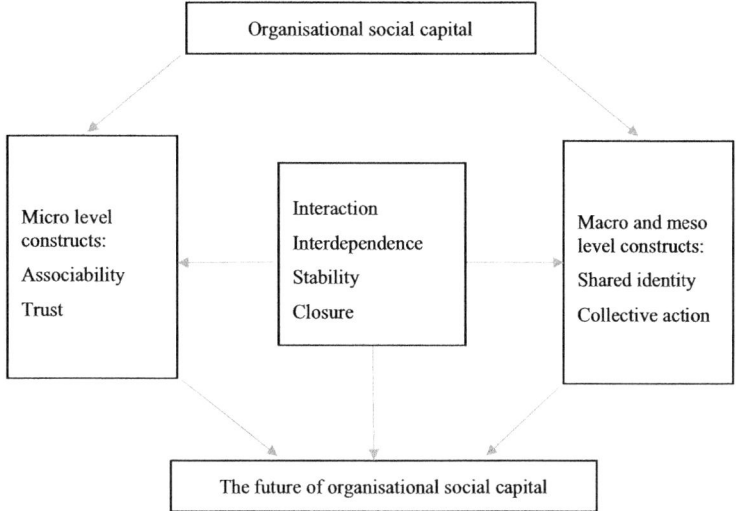

Fig. 1.2 Research framework

Our findings suggest that organisational culture places a strong emphasis on meaningful and informal interactions, fostering a social environment through various events and online platforms. The shift to a hybrid work model, post-pandemic, has prompted the organisation to recognise the evolving nature of professional connections, especially for newer employees and the younger generation. Overall, the organisational culture in the post-pandemic era incorporates a dynamic and supportive work environment that aligns with employee preferences for a hybrid work model.

Nonetheless, the last section includes insights about the future of virtual organisation and a series of practical managerial recommendations that IT&C managers can implement in the virtual organisations of the future. Considering this, the research offers interventions to "humanise" or engage with and improve processes in remote work, including receiving virtual leadership training, developing trust and healthy online culture. In the end, what this research has shown is adaptability, proactive communication and a complete perspective around employee well-being, building an effective corporate culture.

This study also advances the understanding of the use of OSC in the IT&C sector by highlighting its critical role in creating successful teams in remote and hybrid work environments. Based on the theories of Leana and Van Buren (1999) and Nahapiet and Ghoshal (1998), as well as new empirical studies (van Bakel & Horak, 2024), the research demonstrates how these constructs impact team dynamics, particularly by fostering an environment of trust and collective action. Additionally, the study combines a theoretical framework with practical analysis, which could help business experts and managers implement more effective social capital development strategies in virtual and hybrid enterprises and organisations across different sectors and industries.

References

Adam, F., & Rončević, B. (2003). Social capital: Recent debates and trends. *Social Science Information, 42*, 115–183. https://doi.org/10.1177/05390184030420020001

Adler, P. S., & Kwon, S.W. (2002). Social capital: Prospects for a new concept. *The Academy of Management Review, 27*(1), 17–40.

Ajith, M. M., Lux, A. A., Bentley, T., & Striepe, M. (2024). Adaptive crisis management at the operational level: Responses to COVID-19 in the Australian resources sector. *Journal of Management and Organization*, 1–25.

Amonarriz, C. A., Iturrioz, C., Narvaiza, L., & Parrilli, M. D. (2019). The role of social capital in regional innovation systems: Creative social capital and its institutionalization process. *Papers in Regional Science, 98*(1), 35–52.

Arregle, J. L., Hitt, M. A., Sirmon, D. G., & Very, P. (2007). The development of organizational social capital: Attributes of family firms. *Journal of Management Studies, 44*(1), 73–95.

Battilana, J., Sengul, M., Pache, A. C., & Jacob Model, J. (2015). Harnessing productive tensions in hybrid organisations: The case of work integration social enterprises. *Academy of Management Journal, 58*(6), 1658–1685. https://doi.org/10.5465/amj.2013.0903

Ben Hador, B. (2017). Three levels of organisational social capital and their connection to performance. *Journal of Management Development, 36*(3), 348–360.

Bhatti, S. H., Vorobyev, D., Zakariya, R., & Christofi, M. (2020). Social capital, knowledge sharing, work meaningfulness and creativity: Evidence from the Pakistani pharmaceutical industry. *Journal of Intellectual Capital, 22*(2), 243–259.

Bird, M. (2021). Remaking the workspace to boost social connection. *MIT Sloan Management Review, 63*(1), 1–3.

Braun, V., & Clarke, V. (2006). Using thematic analysis in psychology. *Qualitative Research in Psychology, 3*(2), 77–101.
Cantín, L. N., Arrieta, F., Viciano, C. G., & Amonarriz, C. A. (2021). How can small and medium-sized organisations with hybrid objectives preserve their mission? A social capital approach. *REVESCO: Revista de Estudios Cooperativos, 139,* 41–50.
Carmona-Lavado, A., Cuevas-Rodríguez, G., & Cabello-Medina, C. (2010). Social and organisational capital: Building the context for innovation. *Industrial Marketing Management, 39*(4), 681–690.
Cervero-Liceras, F., McKee, M., & Legido-Quigley, H. (2015). The effects of the financial crisis and austerity measures on the Spanish health care system: A qualitative analysis of health professionals' perceptions in the region of Valencia. *Health Policy, 119*(1), 100–106.
Cots, E. G. (2011). Stakeholder social capital: A new approach to stakeholder theory. *Business Ethics: A European Review, 20*(4), 328–341. https://doi.org/10.1111/j.1467-8608.2011.01635.x
Dan, S., Ivana, D., Zaharie, M., Metz, D., & Drăgan, M. (2021). *Digital talent management, insights from the information technology and communication industry.* Palgrave Macmillan.
Dess, G. G., & Shaw, J. D. (2001). Voluntary turnover, social capital, and organisational performance. *The Academy of Management Review, 26*(3), 446.
Erdreich, L. (2024). Social capital practices for the accomplishment of natural-growth: Theoretical insights from low-income mothers' support of remote-learning during COVID. *British Journal of Sociology of Education,* 1–17.
Feitosa, J., Grossman, R., Kramer, W. S., & Salas, E. (2020). Measuring team trust: A critical and meta-analytical review. *Journal of Organisational Behavior, 41*(5), 479–501.
Freeman, R. E., Wicks, A. C., & Parmar, B. (2004). Stakeholder theory and "the corporate objective revisited". *Organisation Science, 15*(3), 364–369.
Greenaway, K. H., Wright, R. G., Willingham, J., Reynolds, K. J., & Haslam, S. A. (2014). Shared identity is key to effective communication. *Personality and Social Psychology Bulletin, 41*(2), 171–182. https://doi.org/10.1177/0146167214559709
Hafermalz, E., & Riemer, K. (2020). Interpersonal connectivity work: Being there with and for geographically distant others. *Organization Studies, 41*(12), 1627–1648.
Hasenfeld, Y., & Gidron, B. (2005). Understanding multi-purpose hybrid voluntary organisations: The contributions of theories on civil society, social movements and non-profit organisations. *Journal of Civil Society, 1*(2), 97–112.

Hassard, J., & Morris, J. (2024). Is managerial homeworking new? Assessing strategic, technological and political influences before, during and after coronavirus. *Organization Studies*, *45*(6), 777–800.

Hausknecht, J. P., & Trevor, C. O. (2011). Collective turnover at the group, unit, and organisational levels: Evidence, issues, and implications. *Journal of Management*, *37*(1), 352–388.

European Union. (2020). JRC120945: Telework in the EU before and after the COVID-19: where we were, where we head to. https://joint-research-centre.ec.europa.eu/system/files/2021-06/jrc120945_policy_brief_-_covid_and_telework_final.pdf

Kellogg, K. (2021). Why workplace hierarchies matter in skill transformation. *MIT Sloan Management Review*, *63*(1), 1–3.

Leana, C. R., & van Buren, H. J. (1999). Organisational social capital and employment practices. *The Academy of Management Review*, *24*(3), 538–555.

Lenz, L., Hattke, F., Kalucza, J., & Redlbacher, F. (2023). Virtual work as a job demand? Work Behaviors of public servants during Covid-19. *Public Performance and Management Review*, *46*(6), 1382–1412.

Mahajan, R., Lim, W. M., Sareen, M., Kumar, S., & Panwar, R. (2023). Stakeholder theory. *Journal of Business Research*, *166*, 114104.

Mayring, P. (2002). *Einführung in die qualitative Sozialforschung: eine Anleitung zu qualitativem Denken*. Beltz Verlag.

Naeem, M., Ozuem, W., Howell, K., & Ranfagni, S. (2023). A step-by-step process of thematic analysis to develop a conceptual model in qualitative research. *International Journal of Qualitative Methods*, *22*, 16094069231205789.

Nahapiet, J., & Ghoshal, S. (1998). Social capital, intellectual capital, and the organisational advantage. *The Academy of Management Review*, *23*(2), 242–266.

Perez Fernandez, H., Rodriguez Escudero, A. I., Martin Cruz, N., & Delgado Garcia, J. B. (2024). The impact of social capital on entrepreneurial intention and its antecedents: Differences between social capital online and offline. *BRQ Business Research Quarterly*, *27*(4), 365–388. https://doi.org/10.1177/23409444211062228

Roman, R. E. C., & Smida, A. (2015). The formation of organisational social capital into technology-based micro enterprises. *Contaduría y Administración*, *60*, 57–81. https://doi.org/10.1016/j.cya.2015.08.009

Rozkwitalska-Welenc, M. (2024). Informal learning in new ways of working. *WSB Journal of Business and Finance*, *58*(1), 73–79.

Ruiz-Ortega, M. J., Parra-Requena, G., García-Villaverde, P. M., & Rodrigo-Alarcon, J. (2017). How does the closure of interorganisational relationships affect entrepreneurial orientation? *BRQ Business Research Quarterly*, *20*(3), 178–191. https://doi.org/10.1016/j.brq.2017.04.003

Rupcic, N. (2024). Working and learning in a hybrid workplace: Challenges and opportunities. *The Learning Organisation, 31*(2), 276–283.

Sanchez-Famoso, V., Maseda, A., Iturralde, T., Danes, S. M., & Aparicio, G. (2019). The potential of internal social capital in organisations: An assessment of past research and suggestions for the future. *Journal of Small Business Management, 58*(1), 32–72.

Sen, S., & Cowley, J. (2012). The relevance of stakeholder theory and social capital theory in the context of CSR in SMEs: An Australian perspective. *Journal of Business Ethics, 118*(2), 413–427. https://doi.org/10.1007/s10 551-012-1598-6

Vaduva, S., & Neagoie, D. (2016). Surviving and thriving in the global economic crisis: The journey and potential of the Romanian IT&C sector. *Procedia— Social and Behavioral Sciences, 221*, 203–210. https://doi.org/10.1016/j.sbs pro.2016.05.107

van Bakel,. M., & Horak, S. (2024). Social capital theory. In K. In Hutchings, S. Michailova, & A. Wilkinson (Eds.), *A guide to key theories for human resource management research* (pp. 261–267). Edward Elgar. https://doi.org/10.4337/9781035308767.ch33

Van Dick, R., Ciampa, V., & Liang, S. (2018). Shared identity in organisational stress and change. *Current Opinion in Psychology, 23*, 20–25.

Villacé-Molinero, T., Fuentes-Moraleda, L., & González-Sánchez, R. (2024). Please don't go: Gendered formal and informal tools for talent retention in hospitality from an organizational social capital approach. *Tourism Management Perspectives, 53*, 101297. https://doi.org/10.1016/j.tmp.2024.101297

CHAPTER 2

Structural Elements of Organisational Social Capital

Abstract To examine the real-world application of the theoretical model, this chapter, as well as Chapter 3, uses a case study methodology. It offers a complex analysis of the IT&C sector in five Romanian cities within one of the top 10 worldwide IT&C companies that successfully handled the shift to remote and hybrid work. The chapter examines, based on existing OSC literature, the macro, meso and micro structural elements of OSC. The macro and meso structural elements of OSC are shared identity and collective action and the microlevel structural elements of OSC are associability and trust. The results are organised by analysing the meaning of each element of OSC by using examples and quotes from the interviews.

Keywords Structural elements of OSC · Research design · Key findings

2.1 Research Design and Methods

We engaged in qualitative interview research (Mayring, 2002), encompassing 33 employees of a large-sized company (from now on referred to as: DATA-CO) acting in the IT&C sector. The company offers a wide range of services including development and integration of customised software solutions, application management testing, IT consultancy, cybersecurity, as well as cloud and AI solutions. The business profile of the

© The Author(s), under exclusive license to Springer Nature
Switzerland AG 2025
D. Ivana et al., *The Dynamics of Social Capital in Romania's IT&C Sector*, https://doi.org/10.1007/978-3-032-01874-8_2

company focuses on offshoring and outsourcing activities. With currently around 2000 staff members (regular employees and contractual staff), the company had a steady growth in the past decade.

This company was selected for the study due to its status as one of the largest IT&C companies in the country, with branches across five cities in Romania and its affiliation with one of the top 10 global IT service providers. For three consecutive years, it has been recognised as a leading employer brand, known for fostering a robust organisational culture centred on trust and responsiveness to employee needs. Over time, the company has introduced innovative human resource development programmes, offering remote work options even prior to the pandemic, designing collaborative workspaces inspired by Silicon Valley and implementing non-financial benefits to enhance employee well-being and promote a balanced work-life environment.

All interviews were structured and conducted based on an interview guideline developed by the three main researchers. The interview guide (see Appendix 1 Interview Question Matrix) consists of 28 questions and includes five sections:

1. Four original factors (stability/time, interaction, interdependence and closure) influencing the creation of OSC covered in questions Q1-Q11.
2. Two additional factors (hybrid work and staff turnover) influencing the flow and stock of OSC covered by questions Q12-Q15.
3. Organisational-level constructs of OSC covered in questions Q16-Q17.
4. Individual-level constructs of OSC addressed by questions Q18-Q23.
5. Organisational Social Capital of the future and future scenarios addressed in questions Q24-Q28.

To reach an accurate and representative pool of professionals for our case study and given the focus of our research on Organisational Social Capital at DATA-CO, we selected the interviewees based on their relevance. All selected interviewees were involved in the People Experience Initiative (henceforth PEM), which is a programme developed by DATA-CO to enhance the level of social activity, bonding and shared identity between company employees. Thus, with the help of two DATA-CO managers involved in the PEM initiative, who identified and contacted the participants and organised the interview settings, we succeeded in carrying out 33 interviews. The interviews took place online in English (32 interviews) and Romanian (1 interview) between February and March 2023. Interviewees provided their consent to participate in the recorded discussions prior to the interviews. They were thoroughly informed about the role, scope and duration of interviews, as well as the language. Demographic information was collected strictly for research purposes. The research team assured the participants of data anonymity and obtained a research ethics approval provided by the Scientific Council of Babeș-Bolyai University before the data collection process started. To further ensure that the study participants feel confident, comfortable and safe, the interviews were held by one of the two members of the research team who had no functional relation to DATA-CO.

The duration of the interviews was 66 minutes on average. The interviews were fully recorded and transcribed, while personal and company-related data were anonymised. We stopped extending our sample when thematic saturation was reached, i.e. neither new significant themes (Almeida & Fernando, 2017, 890; Kane & Levina, 2017, 547) nor new categories (Almeida et al., 2017, 1953; Hopfgartner et al., 2022, 306) emerged during the interviews. We conducted a qualitative content analysis of the interview data (Boréus & Bergström, 2017; Schreier, 2017). We also consulted company documents related to the values of the DATA-CO and the documentation available on the PEM initiative. The system of coding categories emerged in a deductive way: the coding categories are based on the questions from the interview guidelines.

Study Group and Data Analysis

We interviewed 17 women and 16 men, 28 to 58 years old, with an average seniority of about six years. With respect to their job responsibilities, 15 stated that employee management falls within their duties whereas 18 do not have an employee management role. All interviewees have at least a university degree: 12 hold a bachelor's degree, 17 a master's degree and four a doctorate. Regarding their social status, we observe heterogeneity among the interviewees, 11 being married/in a relationship/not in a relationship, with children, and 22 not having children. A tabular representation of the above data is summarised in Table 2.1.

Table 2.1 Demographic dataset

Encoding	Education	Position	Age	Gender
I1	Master's degree	Institutional relations manager	36	Male
I2	Bachelor's degree	AMS consultant	29	Male
I3	Bachelor's degree	Human resources manager	40	Female
I4	Bachelor's degree	Competence Centre manager	32	Male
I5	Master's degree	Competence Centre manager	37	Male
I6	Master's degree	Project Management officer	31	Male
I7	Bachelor's degree	Business analyst	47	Male
I8	Bachelor's degree	Manager	41	Male
I9	Doctorate	Planning and operation manager	38	Female
I10	Bachelor's degree	Software developer	40	Male
I11	Master's degree	Delivery manager and project manager	45	Female
I12	Master's degree	Product manager	49	Female
I13	Master's degree	QA Lead	50	Female
I14	Doctorate	Business analyst	35	Female
I15	Master's degree	Developer	32	Female
I16	Master's degree	Business developer	40	Female
I17	Bachelor's degree	People experience manager	33	Female
I18	Masters	Salesforce developer	28	Female
I19	Master's degree	Talent acquisition manager	33	Female
I20	Bachelor's degree	Business developer	35	Female
I21	Master's degree	Team Lead consultant project manager officer	33	Female
I22	Bachelor's degree	Programmer	28	Male
I23	Doctorate	CHRO	42	Female
I24	Bachelor's degree	Team manager	34	Male
I25	Doctorate	Business developer	40	Male
I26	Master's degree	Quality system manager	40	Female
I27	Master's degree	Team manager	33	Male
I28	Master's degree	Team manager	34	Male
I29	Master's degree	Competence Centre manager	38	Male
I30	Bachelor's degree	Project manager	48	Male
I31	Bachelor's degree	Project manager	58	Male
I32	Master's degree	Team manager	36	Female
I33	Master's degree	Talent acquisition manager	36	Female

The following criteria have been selected in terms of purposeful sampling composition:

1. job seniority.

2. active involvement in the PEM initiative.
3. balanced representation of managerial and non-managerial roles.
4. balanced representation of both men and women.

Before the interviews, we also analysed historical documents (between 2013 and 2022) regarding the structural differences between participants' human resource characteristics. Thus, several conclusions could be drawn in preparing the interviews:

- First of all, the number of freelancers has increased considerably over the years, particularly starting with 2017 (from 9 in 2013 to over 600 in 2019 and over 500 in 2022). Freelancers have a service contract with the company, but they operate individually and do not depend on DATA-CO legally and logistically. They may have multiple contracts with several companies at the same time, and therefore, their connection to DATA-CO is less strong than that of regular employees. It is important to note that starting with 2017, freelancers make up about a third of the total number of employees, which has implications for the OSC of the company and the organisational culture more generally, given their distinct status and weak connection to the company (despite DATA-CO's efforts to integrate them within the company).
- Secondly, the number of employees (apart from freelancers) has increased three times since 2013 (from 403 in 2013 to 1223 in 2022). This also has direct implications for the OSC and organisational values as it is more difficult to adopt and internalise values when the number of employees increases so significantly. This is particularly the case given the changes in values and work practices brought about by the change of ownership and later and more recently by the rapid increase in hybrid and remote work.
- Thirdly, and most importantly for our purposes, the turnover rate has fluctuated over the years but has had the tendency to increase over the past years particularly starting with 2021 (over 27% compared to 14% in 2020). This rate, however, is the gross rate that includes both regular employees and the freelancers. As mentioned before, freelancers are only partially connected to the company, and if we refer only to the turnover rate of regular employees, then it increases

significantly (37% in 2022 compared to 21% in 2013 and 19% in 2017).

It is important to note that these rates are not specific only to DATA-CO as they reflect more general trends in the IT&C industry in Romania. At the same time, however, the frequent changes in personnel have key implications for the creation and consolidation of OSC and building the future organisational culture in the post-pandemic world marked by uncertainty. In terms of our conceptualisation of OSC, it is expected that turnover will affect closure and OSC negatively as it creates difficulty in internalising the company's organisational values.

The data were analysed by following a qualitative methodology. Several steps were carried out within the coding process:

1. a weight filter on a scale from 1 to 100 where 100 means a very valuable coded segment.
2. coding comments, destined to provide additional instructions on how to interpret data to code on an accurate deductive basis.
3. continuous adjusting of the coding scheme by creating/enlarging/merging codes and sub-codes.

We conducted an intercoder agreement process, which is the most frequently used method, where the coders code the data material independently of each other and then compare their results (Rädiker & Kuckartz, 2019), followed by the final agreement upon the coding scheme and the initial dataset. A minimum of two independent coders is necessary to estimate intercoder reliability, which is a good practice within qualitative research while allowing transparency, systematicity and communicability (O'Connor & Joffe, 2020).

The output of the percentage level can be interpreted using the same benchmark notes on Cohen's kappa where we speak of a good ("substantial") result from 61% and of a very good result from 81% ("almost perfect") (Rädiker & Kuckartz, 2019). Thus, the coding scheme was initially developed upon the interview guideline and continuously adjusted through five rounds of intercoder agreement (i.e. 5 interviews) until it reached its final form agreed by both coders (13 themes encompassing 140 codes), after agreeing upon the final coding scheme and ensuring an almost perfect intercoder agreement per cent (95,06%).

Further on, each coder separately coded 14 interviews, resulting in 2204 coded segments.

2.2 Key Findings

2.2.1 Macrolevel Structural Elements of OSC

Shared Identity.
Within the section regarding the primary code shared identity, we identified mixed impressions among the interviewees. Management and coaching team representatives indicate that building up a shared identity has been and is still an ongoing preoccupation. Overall, interviewees perceive the shared organisational identity ranging from very low to high, with some indicating that reaching the financial goals of the company would be one of the few reasons for shared identity: "I don't know any other common goal than making money for the company" (I22), whereas senior employees believe that this is one aspect that is fostered when people are working together for a longer period of time: "So, when we work with people who have been with the company for more than five years, there is already a sense of knowing our goals, our experience, and we rely on each other. Therefore, definitely, in that group of people who have been working together for a long time, there is this common organisational identity, we know what this company stands for. We have adapted our values accordingly for new employees in the organisation, because the organisation has also changed [..]" (I26). Also, one interviewee indicated that newcomers encounter challenges in building up a shared identity, if their activity lacks an active interaction at the office.

Regarding the shared identity sub-code none, we grasped interviewees' perception regarding the explicit lack of it: "To some extent, but we still have work to do in this regard. I don't think there is a common identity. I mean, everyone assumes their own identity or contribution. I don't think they have a common understanding or that they understand the same beliefs in the same way" (I8). Thus, interviewees state that shared identity cannot be nurtured while some employees jump from one project to the next. Also, a great focus on client to the detriment of employees: "Apart from 'the client comes first', I don't know exactly what the company's objectives are" (I21), senior managers failing to integrate newcomers, employees having only a financial goal in mind, contribute to this perception of a non-existing shared identity.

With respect to shared identity with the organisation, most interviewees perceive this in a positive way, meaning that working together to reach common objectives, contributing to client satisfaction and being part of a larger holding group, on an international level, adds up to this feeling: "I would rate it very positively. And it is also related to the previous question, the fact that we are part of an international group and that there is an employer brand, and we feel this very strongly in different ways, it makes us feel that we are part of a larger organisation, not just one limited to our country, our branch, or our specific location. It also helps us access knowledge. And also, as I was saying in relation to the previous questions, the way we manage changes in the labour market, the fact that we are part of an international group helps us access expertise, training, or knowledge from across the organisation, which is larger than our company. [...]" (I16). However, as with the opinions expressed above, this perception of a positive common identity with the organisation is predominantly felt by long-serving employees.

Regarding the shared identity with the team, interviewees state that they have experienced this feeling more within their teams/groups/microcultures, attributing this to the beneficial synergy of collaborating towards similar objectives and fostering personal connections: "[...] There is now a new concept called microcultures. Consequently, I don't think we can talk about a single organisational culture anymore. Another effect of the pandemic is that people are now building their own cultures in smaller teams. They also create the environment and everything they need to feel comfortable at work at all times of the day. So, from my perspective, we have many microcultures today, and in the culture diagnosis we did, we noticed that people say they feel very comfortable in their teams. And they don't care what happens above them. That's microculture: things can change, hierarchies can change, managers can change, but in their little universe, they feel good. And, in fact, they don't care what happens outside. That's microculture" (I23). At the same time, there are interviewees who perceive that not all teams might feel this shared identity, mainly because of being part of a very large organisation and own beliefs and values, that might or might not align with company's ones.

Collective Action.
Collective action refers to the ability of organisational members (managers, colleagues) to act collectively for common goals (doing things together for a common purpose). Thus, we investigated collective action

from two viewpoints, namely social groups (24 segments) and team level (26 segments). Interviewees perceive the two perspectives very similar, whereas most of them (over 50%) have positive examples regarding collective action. They remember some sources of collective action such as communities for sport, social action and cultural initiatives (such as a book club), which are on a voluntary basis and are distributed via the internal communication channels. There are also few employees that report lack of collective action in social groups motivating that "everybody is here for themselves" or "but it's not like let's do that together"; be that as it may, it seems that collective action in social groups originates at department and team level, and is mostly attributed to the line manager's responsibilities: "those managers are doing their best to create a good collective". Some negative perspectives are also being shared, while interviewees state that they "lack the bigger picture", and "everybody sees their own business in their own struggles".

On a team level, the perceived collective action is also reported in most of the segments, while the common interest of the project is the source of overlap with all the individual interests of team members. Thus, the teams share a unified objective to fulfil client requirements and in order to do so, individual goals align for the "common good". When debated if collective action is a general feeling on an organisational level, there are viewpoints where it is clearly stated that collective action functions better on team and department level and, if several departments are involved, the feeling dilutes: "When multiple departments are involved, it doesn't work as well. Even if they want to and even if they try. Yes. For some reason, it doesn't work" (I10). One interviewee observes a missing procedure which could support collective action: "And, of course, everyone wants to achieve the goal. The problem is that, in the case of collective action, what we lack, I would say, is a working method; in other words, everyone wants the job done, but we don't have a clear plan (…) So even if we want to do it and we have the same goal, we don't necessarily work in a very organised way. In some cases, just as some headless chickens" (I29).

2.2.2 Microlevel Structural Elements of OSC

Associability.
Associability can be considered as a mixed bundle of perceptions. Regarding any neutral, positive or negative assumptions, we could notice a very tight score. Interviewee testimonials suggest that collective goals

have to be aligned with personal ones in order to succeed, or as trying to fulfil own goals while still meeting organisational aims: "Surely one can see it that way, but there are of course situations in which one is busy with other activities that need to be done on that day, let's say, and naturally one tends to give priority to one's daily obligations, or let's say, the core tasks one has, rather than a common goal at a specific point in time" (I11). Nevertheless, younger employees tend to prioritise their own goals: "I would say that it is not very good. But I think it depends on age; young people see or give priority to personal interests, while older people give priority to collective interests" (I10). Another interviewee considers that collective actions help to reach a company's goals, not individual goals. Colleagues in managerial roles tend to prioritise common goals more: "I think the manager or managers focus more on the organisational aspect. That is, managers focus more on teamwork" (I14). However, we found evidence in the narrations that some managers do not wish to further invest in the relationship with their colleagues. At the same time, there are colleagues who choose not to be involved in reaching common goals due to personal priorities. The degree of associability has also proven to depend on seniority level, and thus, it is built over time and influenced by the managers' direct engagement.

Trust
Trust as a largely addressed topic mainly referred to trust of employees doing their work. Also, trust was understood as being related to transparency: "[...] When it comes to trust, we talked about transparency in the first part of our meeting. We can't have transparency without trust, and since we don't have that kind of transparency at some levels, I don't think we have trust. Okay", (I7) but also trust in managing the company's hardware. One interviewee stated that people started to trust their managers more, but there still were teams with a great lack of trust. Senior colleagues have the courage to state what would not or is not fulfilled on a trust level. Other interviewees merely expressed the hope that trust existed. Regarding the potential influence of hybrid work on how trust manifests itself, it is the opinion of the interviewees that people who did their work well before the pandemic also performed well when working from home. According to some statements, at the beginning of the pandemic, managers did not have a sufficient level of trust on how colleagues performed their tasks, resulting in micromanagement (not trusting colleagues enough to do their job).

Trust among individuals can be categorised into fragile, resilient and generalised forms, illuminating how trust is perceived at all levels, whether between coworkers or between colleagues and managers. While coded valences seem to have an almost even distribution, statements regarding a fragile trust refer to the existence of trust rather on microlevels, the tendency to be cautious, working fully remote and thus not being able to bond at the desired level. One interviewee perceived that remote employment during pandemic greatly affected the level of trust that existed before: "Trust is very fragile at the moment. Before the pandemic, I would say there was long-term confidence. And things were, of course, different, better, I would say. But at the moment, I think confidence is very short-term" (I4). However, one interviewee acknowledges that part of the decision in becoming a manager was to actually drive change in these aspects. The degree of trust also depends on the individuals with whom the interviewees interact, and thus an associated level of fragile trust would be strictly related to the persons they interact with. Also, a fragile trust resulted in promises that never materialised or is linked to expectations strictly on a transactional basis, for example being reassigned on a new project, receiving a monthly pay cheque, etc. A resilient trust between people was identified by employees who have been in the company for a longer period, a perception influenced by social relationships, achieved results and grounded in integrity and fairness: "I think it's based on integrity, which means that everyone knows how to do their job. And I think that when you join a company, everyone believes that you are fair, that you do your job correctly. And this is by default; no one will check very, very carefully whether you are fair or not. That is implicit. And for me, that is a very, very good thing and a very good value for granting trust […]" (I9). Generalised trust is being perceived as a high level of trust between colleagues and managers, both vertically and horizontally. According to interviewees, this category of trust has been improved over time.

In matters of trust in the organisation as a whole entity, a fragile trust was described when referring to branches distributed within other locations, and to managers and the leadership team as a whole, the latter being also related to expectations or promises that were not (entirely) met. The last few years, marked by several insecurities, also contributed to a decreased level of trust: "I don't think everyone trusts the organisation, at this point. As I mentioned, there have been many changes in recent years. Yes, we are becoming more stable every day. But people have started to lose trust in the organisation, probably because of the financial situation in our country" (I4).

In addition, being unable as an employee without any managerial function to fully understand a company's strategies and future endeavours leads to a lower degree of trust. Further statements enforce the characteristics of a strictly transactional relationship. Again, newcomers are seen as needing more time to build up a steadier trust relationship. A resilient trust in the organisation as a whole entity refers to experiencing difficulties and differences over time, but also to overcoming them, hence people must find solutions within the organisation to ensure continuity: "But, on the other hand, we have encountered obstacles and managed to overcome them. So, in terms of resilience, I am confident that we can find solutions within the organisation to ensure continuity. That is why I said it is somewhere in between, because it depends on the market" (I28). Interviewees who experience a resilient trust also state that trust is ongoing, or no (major) disappointments occurred over time. Hence, resilient trust is perceived as a consequence of being part of a resilient company that managed to navigate through various types of crises. Also, another reason is represented by the values of the company that are in line with some employee values. Further on, (re)assuring messages on behalf of the CEO contributed to sustaining and ensuring a resilient level of trust. In addition, one interviewee states that being aware of the existence of a thorough HR recruitment and selection process also ensures a higher degree of trust in the company. A diversified service portfolio also contributes to a resilient trust. Again, employees with a higher seniority might experience resilient trust, compared to newcomers.

A generalised trust in the organisation as a whole entity is marked (according to some interviewees) by the Japanese culture, thus ensuring a safe, respectful environment: "Certainly, as I mentioned, the first feeling of trust comes from the fact that we belong to a Japanese company and that employees feel secure with their jobs. Especially at this moment, they really appreciate being part of a company that does not appear in the newspapers, where it is written that no one knows who will be laid off and who will not. So, the overall level of trust comes from the fact that we guarantee their jobs" (I23). Also, interviewees mention the opportunities for development within the company. The large size of the company is also perceived as an indicator of a generalised trust. Trust in individuals who form the top management has also been mentioned, mainly because of the perception according to which decisions are fact based and there is a long-term vision. However, the level of trust is also strongly related to the seniority level and an existing managerial position.

Regarding trust between colleagues, only a few statements suggest that it is entirely absent or fragile, mainly due to perceived feelings of unreliability and dishonesty. Even so, most coded segments address resilient trust, and interviewees assert that cultivating friendships with colleagues fosters trust, which is based on fulfilling promises, maintaining transparency and being present: "Personally, I have a very good relationship with my colleagues. Usually, such good relationship at work translates into a good relationship outside of work, which means that we trust each other to discuss other things and become, let's say, best friends, friends, work colleagues, and yes, colleagues with whom I interact socially outside of work teams. I feel that when we work together, we work better" (I25). One interviewee stated that this relationship based on trust remained even after the colleague left the company: "And I have the same kind of trust in other colleagues, in former colleagues who have left the company. We had this trust when they were in the company, and we still have it after they left" (I7). Furthermore, being present in person, at the office, fosters a stronger connection between colleagues both according to interviewees, whether they hold a managerial position or not. Transparency and honesty, willingness to support and help each other, providing feedback and offering assistance, mentoring each other, trust in colleagues' abilities, and openness in discussing any topic (both work and non-work related), were also underlined as being of utmost importance. The level of seniority and a common history among colleagues also ensured this level of resilient trust. Generalised trust between interviewees and colleagues highlighted mainly fostering trust and the benefit of doubt, entrusting problems and issues to a safe environment and trying to figure out solutions. Regarding trust between interviewees and their manager, some testimonials describe this as fragile because of a lack of trust in the upper leadership team, lack of communication, withholding truths, feeling unappreciated or not considered as an employee, or managers not fighting enough for their people: "Okay, great. I was saying that the trust I have in my human resources manager is fragile. I asked my manager questions, making considerable efforts to receive objective and professional answers, without any personal bias. Therefore, I feel that my manager does not have confidence in my abilities, does not believe that I can contribute consistently to the company and the technical team I am part of. I feel like struggling here" (I14). One interviewee also indicated that managers altering duties and priorities during projects contributed to a sense of fragile trust. Changes in leadership over the last years generated for one interviewee the perception of new managers that are less people oriented.

Resilient trust was described as feeling comfortable with each other. People with a high seniority level trust their managers and at the same time withhold a managerial position themselves and describe the relationship as being open and productive. Trusting their manager's decisions in difficult situations was also mentioned: "So, this also applies to my manager. I think that when I need advice or find myself in a situation I haven't been in before, I find something I haven't found before, I go to my manager, I feel comfortable talking to her and asking for her advice or opinion, and I always get an excellent answer or something that really helps me in that situation" (I17). One interviewee describes the relationship with the manager as a form of professional attachment, whereas another interviewee states that the manager genuinely cares about the team's well-being. Working together for common goals and backing up each other were also mentioned.

With respect to generalised trust between interviewees and their manager, interviewees mention that receiving guidance, solutions and recommendations, taking employees' needs and requirements into account builds up this kind of trust with the manager: "I see that, over time, even though they have changed, they try to take my needs into account, not just mine, but in general, managers try to take into account the needs of the people they coordinate. And in my case, I also try to take their needs into account. Therefore, we reach a compromise, we support each other in one way or another" (I10). In addition, keeping the manager informed about general issues related to work or personal issues that might affect work is kind of a matter of common sense on behalf of one interviewee. Also, receiving support from the manager when initiating their own idea, even when and if the outcome is not as expected, would further reinforce trust.

References

Almeida, S., & Fernando, M. (2017). Making the cut: occupation-specific factors influencing employers in their recruitment and selection of immigrant professionals in the information technology and accounting occupations in regional

Australia. *International Journal of Human Resource Management, 28*(6), 880–912.

Boréus, K., & Bergström, G. (2017). *Analysing text and discourse: Eight approaches for the social sciences.* Sage.

Hopfgartner, L., Seubert, C., Sprenger, F., & Glaser, J. (2022). Experiences of precariousness and exploitation of Romanian transnational live-in care workers in Austria. *Journal of Industrial Relations, 64*(2), 298–320.

Kane, A. A., & Levina, N. (2017). 'Am I still one of them?': Bicultural immigrant managers navigating social identity threats when spanning global boundaries. *Journal of Management Studies, 54*(4), 540–577.

Mayring, P. (2002). *Einführung in die qualitative Sozialforschung: eine Anleitung zum qualitativen Denken.* Beltz Verlag.

O'Connor, C., & Joffe, H. (2020). Intercoder reliability in qualitative research: Debates and practical guidelines. *International Journal of Qualitative Methods, 19*, 1–13.

Rädiker, S., & Kuckartz, U. (2019). *Analyse qualitativer Daten mit MAXQDA.* Text, Audio und Video, Springer Verlag.

Schreier, M. (2017). Kontexte qualitativer Sozialforschung: Arts-based research, mixed methods und emergent methods. *Forum Qualitative Sozialforschung/ Forum: Qualitative Social Research, 18*(2), 27.

CHAPTER 3

Organisational Social Capital Influencing Factors

Abstract To continue the framework presented in the previous chapter, this chapter examines the influence of four main factors impacting OSC: interaction, interdependence, stability and closure (Nahapiet & Ghoshal, 1998). Results show that team autonomy is sustained by internal collaboration and client implication, by promoting interdependence between roles. Stability is variably perceived—challenged by organisational changes, communication gaps and turnover, but maintained through dynamic structures and transparent leadership style. Closure emerges as both a structural and emotional process, where sometimes employees express a weak attachment to the company, but a stronger bond to the client. The quality of interaction and common values highlight the identification with the organisation, by underlining the importance of openness and continuity to foster long-term commitment.

Keywords OSC influencing factor · research results

3.1 Influencing Factor Number 1: Interaction

At DATA-CO, strong connections are highly appreciated within the company environment: "I would say that what we try to do in the company is to ensure that the interactions that take place are meaningful… In an informal sense, I just want to see if you are well, if your family is well, to talk about what is happening" (I23).

The culture of the organisation emphasises commitment to deep connections and fosters social engagement. The company facilitates active social interaction among its employees by providing them with the chance to take part in a variety of activities: "Well, I would say that there is a lot of social interaction within the organisation. I would say that there are many opportunities, many options. So, if someone wants to get more involved in the social life of the organisation, they have opportunities, enough opportunities, so yes, there are enough opportunities" (I14). However, a deep engagement in real life requires a steady flow of information. Colleagues should share their perspective and knowledge since it is a source of personal confidence and not only a question of choice: "For me, the problem is that if I don't get enough information from the people I need, I feel very insecure, very uncertain about my presence and position within the company" (I14).

The dynamic of social interaction has evolved in the post-pandemic era. The corporation acknowledges that employee collaboration has evolved from its former condition. A reason for this change is remote work and the lack of a physical common area. Nevertheless, the organisation wants to promote dependency and cooperation: "What I want to say is that there is currently social interaction within our company. But it is very different from what we had before the pandemic in recent years. And I mean that although colleagues are usually influenced by their managers to collaborate, collaboration in our company is still promoted" (I19).

It is important to note that the changing dynamics of social interaction have distinct effects on different generations and groups (juniors and seniors, for example) within the organisation. Younger workers who joined the company after 2020 might not find the traditional workplace culture of camaraderie and collaboration as appealing. The fact that there is a lack of shared physical space has determined them to adopt a different strategy for forming in-office friendships, which illustrated the evolving nature of business relationships: "But the tasks, colleagues, and clients are the most important aspects of the job, because you spend the most time with them and interact with them. If they don't fit, you won't like the job, and you'll experience a lot of frustration. So yes" (I2).

Some people play key roles in these encounters. For example, in the CEO's instance, there is a quick but helpful conversation. Talks are mostly with department heads and other top officials, including the Chief Executive Officer. By means of these conversations, the staff member gains knowledge of the CEO's expectations for the day-to-day management of the business. Furthermore, through these encounters, individuals may provide their unique perspectives on the organisation's aims and programmes and contribute to the decision-making process: "I have had limited but very valuable interactions with our CEO. Most interactions take place with the CEO and department heads. So, at this point, you get to know the CEO's requirements in terms of operations. And, of course, the operational side presents projects or programs, questions, requests. Then you can express your opinion or point of view" (I26).

3.1.1 Forms of Interaction

Organisational changes and evolving workplace dynamics may suggest a transition to a more dynamic and relaxed work environment. Employees tend to desire informality more than just small talk; they want to change the way they engage with their managers: "We have developed several informal communities with different purposes, such as sports, cultural activities, book clubs, and so on, where people can interact in a more informal way" (I23).

Departments reflect a setting represented by both in-person and virtual meetings and shape daily interactions. This hybrid model reflects a further cultural change in the organisation. Managers and other supervisors collaborate outside the workplace to reinforce a culture of cooperative and accessible culture: "I would start with our department, where I am present every day, together with my colleagues, with whom I have a very good relationship" (I24). This statement emphasises the need for open communication that encourages staff members to express concerns and have honest conversations about problems. If this ideal type of communication is achieved, it creates a supportive and courteous atmosphere where ideas are openly exchanged: "I get along very well with all my colleagues, my managers and my team leaders" (I2).

Geographical distance, however, limits the number and kind of social connections that may be enhanced, which might have an impact on team cohesiveness: "Since no one on my team lives in Bucharest, I don't interact much" (I2). But things take a turn for the better when team members gather for social events like Christmas parties and team buildings to new locations, where they have the opportunity to get to know one another. Digital communication has become an important instrument in sustaining the informal part in the organisation. For example, employees use group chats for athletic events on Microsoft Teams, in Bucharest, in order to connect: "We have a Teams group in Bucharest, for example, for sports activities, and everyone posts their interests there" (I2), which reveals a proactive approach to fostering shared interests. These virtual approaches meet the interests of staff members and support diverse group activities, including sports and reading clubs, in addition to strengthening the sense of community.

Thus, as the pandemic's effects became clear, interaction patterns changed significantly: "There is obviously a big difference compared to face-to-face interaction. Before the pandemic, we only worked from the office" (I12). These changes have demonstrated how different the issues that arise from living in a digital world really are, as opposed to what happens when we communicate face-to-face to one another. In order to address this high risk of miscommunication, it is essential to have direct contact with others when enhancing the quality of work life. This is an example of a strategic initiative triggered by the fast-moving nature of virtual collaboration in this organisation: "You know... what we're trying to do is reduce the number of unnecessary meetings and interactions, so that people don't feel exhausted from too many online meetings" (I23).

3.1.2 Benefits and Quality of In-person Interaction

The organisation underlines how the distinctive dynamics of in-person interaction significantly enhance professional relationships. They acknowledge that informal moments such as casual discussions, coffee breaks and shared lunches enhance the depth and authenticity of these connections. This perspective highlights the human touch and warmth that physical interaction brings to professional communication, recognising the unique element of in-person interactions: "And I think that the relationship, the connection, the bond with my colleagues when I go to the office is somehow different, because we have the opportunity to talk face to face, have a coffee together, or have lunch together" (I7). Employees who opt to spend more time at the office contribute to a more dynamic social atmosphere, where interactions move beyond the work-related tasks or business challenges. Due to the diverse range of topics and interactions that take place in a physical context, this environment promotes an environment that feels both vibrant and multidimensional, all thanks to the positive social energy cultivated within the physical space: "So, when people come to the office, there is quite good social interaction, discussions about things other than strictly work-related issues or problems or business, as usual" (I25).

3.1.3 Input from Clients, Managers and Colleagues

The way a team works in the company changes when a developer explains how people interact. The whole team becomes the main structure, with a focus on reaching out to team members, the product owner, for input and questions. It is important to note that there are situations of reduced interaction with company colleagues and more engagement with the client. This situation is an example of how relationships are spread out in complex ways at the workplace, and it suggests that people choose to increase energy for team connections and working with clients: "And one of the developers who is part of the team is there. Yes, when we need the product owner, when we need information or have questions, we generally go to them. So, I interact less with my colleague at DATA-CO and more with the client" (I10).

In some circumstances, collaborating with the manager responsible for client projects requires to support the administrative and financial dimensions of project management. This role needs to be flexible enough to handle changes in the project, organisation or team, changes that might come as unexpected for some people. The process of adjustment is facilitated by the manager and coworkers, who are a few of the many information sources within the company, which help making the transition smoother. Also, they bring out the collaborative aspect of the position and the necessity to remain informed about modifications, maybe with support from peers. This means that previous experience of staff members is seen as a valuable foundation to meet the role's requirements: "My daily tasks are related to project management assistance. Basically, I work very closely with my senior manager, who delivers the project to our end client. I support them with some project management aspects, administrative and financial tasks, so that when changes occur in the team or in the organisation, or even better in the project, I am informed by them. I mean, they are not the only person, there are several, and they keep us informed. In this case, I have to adapt and make the necessary changes to be able to continue. From time to time, I also get help from my colleagues. Before that, yes, I had some previous experience, which helped me quite a lot in this role" (I6).

A collaborative atmosphere is achieved among the team when all members are willing to help and exchange information with one another. They respond to questions from fellow professionals at will and even provide additional information when they can. They often cannot respond to a question if they do not have sufficient expertise but defer it to a more informed coworker. The language-switching technique, shown here by switching to German, is used in the story to clarify that we are now talking with another team member (to ask for more information or clarification): "Yes, my colleagues are all willing to help if they have time to answer your question or provide you with more information, or, at the very least, if they are not familiar with the case, they will refer you to the right person. I apologise, I will switch to German, but there is at least one other person you can contact for more information" (I21).

3.2 Influencing Factor Number 2: Interdependence

3.2.1 Functional Interdependence

A team manager outlines the variety of responsibilities, which involves both internal organisational matters and the development of team members, all reflected within the complex network of interdependence that exists within the organisation. This role requires conducting performance reviews and engaging in customised interactions with team members. Furthermore, an additional layer of complexity is identifying project managers for each client, emphasising the necessity of collaboration to address the issues posed by client-specific initiatives: "So, we, I, for example, as a whole, are team managers. Therefore, I am responsible for the internal aspects of the organisation such as the development of colleagues, as I said, individually, but also performance evaluations; however, for each client we also have a project manager" (I28).

As this unfolds, other workers emphasise how they rely on their colleagues to complete tasks for the transition, reflecting the dependencies inherent in their roles. Their daily tasks highlight the interconnections that represent the collaborative essence of their roles. It is noted that despite being part of a larger project or team, there is a sense of independence, with some characterising their role as similar to a "one-man show", where reliance primarily derives from the client or project rather than within the immediate team. Collectively, these narratives bring functional interdependence to the light, showcasing both the individualistic and collaborative parts of the organisational structure.

"It depends, of course, on other colleagues, the transition team, and interdependencies. I will only identify the tasks that are part of their responsibilities, basically the daily tasks they should perform. But other than that, I don't think the question really applies to what we do. Because if we were working on a project, for example, then of course you would interact with other colleagues, because let's say one of them is working on something you are working on, and you need some information, you go to the financial department, exchange information, etc., that's how it works. But because I work more on my own, the interdependence is, of course, only with the client or the project, but not necessarily within the team" (I29).

3.2.2 Relational Interdependence as a Mechanism to Address Turnover and Improve Retention

Certain circumstances highlight the intentional effort necessary to foster shared experiences with colleagues while balancing personal and professional boundaries. For example, proposing a lunch together can strengthen relationships on both personal and professional sides. This project emphasises the fact that professional relationships are holistic, where shared experiences beyond the formal work environment can lead to a deeper appreciation of one another: "But at the same time, we can decide, for example, that tomorrow we will both go to the office, have lunch together, and discuss our professional or personal issues, depending on what kind of conversation we would like to have" (I7).

Several interviewees highlight the importance of having open discussions about personal choices that may impact the workplace atmosphere. Particularly, discussing in an open manner, especially regarding potential departures, reflects a commitment to maintain transparency and clear lines of dialogue. This approach reveals the interplay between professional and personal facets in the workplace, even as the primary motivation remains personal satisfaction within the organisation: "All the time, with these people, I talk about what they like to discuss, and if they like to discuss it with me, we discuss it and come to some kind of understanding. Please tell me personally if you want to leave. Don't let me receive an email announcing that you are leaving the company. And if they want to discuss it with me, I will discuss it with them anytime. I will be open to these kinds of discussions, and I hope they do not leave the company, as I have told you" (I7).

An alternative perspective emphasises the relationship between personal and professional contacts, within a broader organisational structure. It is important to acknowledge that conversations and meetings go beyond just project-related tasks and emphasise the complex nature of workplace relationships. Personal approaches are inherently integrated into the essence of collaboration, with laughter and shared experiences playing an important role in creating a unified working environment: "So, of course, when we discuss something or have meetings to find out something, to carry out a task for a project or something like that, we definitely have personal relationships, so to speak, or we have a certain communication that is not strictly related to the project or task we are carrying out. Of course, we know things about each other, sometimes we laugh, I mean, that's the case for me, I don't know how it is for the others. But yes, we also interact in this area with the people we are connected to, for example, if I am part of a project team that is working, with whom we are working together for a client, on a specific project or preparing a specific project or something like that, we definitely have some personal interactions at some point, because in my role, for example, as a project manager or also as a delivery manager, I have some people I need to follow up with to see if their activities are delivering what they need to deliver" (I11).

Another employee underlines that interdependence extends beyond specific responsibilities. The fact that individuals are fundamentally human, regardless of their responsibilities or duties, highlights that maintaining humanity at the workplace is also important. This perspective values personal connections more than professional ones, acknowledging important milestones and life events in colleagues' lives, which in turn deepen professional relationships by fostering a greater understanding of each person's unique story: "So, before being, I don't know, a project manager or delivery manager or consultant, or I don't know, an accountant responsible for human resources, we are first and foremost human beings. Yes, from my perspective, I have a personal relationship with almost everyone. I know when, you know, my colleague in the accounting department is getting married and things like that" (I11).

3.2.3 Pooled Interdependence

As a team manager explains, the organisation provides intricate dynamics of functional interdependence. Acknowledging colleagues who collaborate on projects for a shared client across various teams and regions reveals a complex network of partnerships. The mention of different team managers and locations underscores the complexity of these relationships. Additionally, team activities specific to certain areas highlight the presence of localised dynamics that work independently, free from direct involvement or interaction. This situation illustrates the intricate web of functional connections, fostering a cooperative work environment influenced by both project needs and regional variations: "And it may happen that some of my colleagues are working on a project for a client that also involves colleagues from other teams. The teams may be located in places such as Brașov or Iași, or they may have a different team manager. The others are grouped together… We have this situation because, in some cases, we also have team activities that are related to a single team or a single location, I would say, over which we have no influence and with which we do not interact" (I28).

In a different context, a member from another company addresses the issue of group autonomy within the client interface. The dispersion of responsibility focuses on teams collaborating autonomously with their clients. The efforts to bring teams together, share personal experiences and highlight lessons learned reflect a proactive approach to maintaining a collaborative environment. The reference to the company's events as venues for gathering reflects a commitment to fostering communication opportunities across teams. These claims illustrate the careful balance between the need for structured connections within the broader organisational framework and the autonomy of individual teams: "They are independent, each team works with the client, but the links between them must be ensured by me or by DATA-CO. We have tried to bring them together to exchange impressions and find out what lessons we can learn, and they also meet at DATA-CO events" (I27).

3.2.4 Sequential Interdependence

The focus is on client feedback, which often develops gradually as the team becomes involved in client projects and emphasises the collaborative nature inherent in the broader project framework. Acknowledging the interplay between different roles highlights the synergy required for successful project implementation. However, the unique aspect manifests as a notable interdependence, particularly in sequential tasks, among team members and those from other teams. This fact provides a comprehensive perspective, highlighting the group's capacity to adapt and function autonomously within the integrated framework: "Most of the input comes in the form of projects from clients, where we need things to happen in sequence because we are integrated into the project, into the client's teams, and into the client's projects. It's a big chain within a project, and there are multiple roles that interact, and we need input from different roles, but that happens rarely. That's why I said that nothing comes to mind. It's rare that we have such a strong dependency, like a sequence, between some members of my team and other members of the team" (I28).

3.2.5 Reciprocal Interdependence

Members of the team depend on one another, establishing interdependencies that are essential for the project's success. This situation emphasises the importance of collaboration within the team, within the context of a project. Consequently, these collaborative dynamics lead to the formation of dependencies, providing evidence of the interdependence that defines successful teamwork: "Hence, colleagues interact with each other. I would say that in a project, if you are part of the same team, at some point you will depend on each other for certain results or information that you provide. So, there is a certain dependency" (I28).

In the complex field of interdependence, the perspective presented underlines the essential collaborative nature of roles. The assertion that contributions from others account for more than 50% of the effort illustrates the inherently interconnected nature of the day-to-day working tasks. Collaborative efforts extend beyond the immediate team, including interactions with other departments such as tax, HR, employee experience and management. This example highlights the importance of teamwork in the workplace and the necessity of different contributions for seamless workflow integration: "In terms of interdependence with other colleagues and managers, the work depends on the contribution of others for more than 50% of the time. Close collaboration takes place with management departments and other colleagues from People Experience, as well as with other human resources and financial departments. This link highlights the interdependence of the work with the contributions of different people" (I17).

Another viewpoint emphasises the importance of collaboration between departments, especially in cases that involve specialised technologies. In order to leverage specific skills within the organisation, a strategic approach would be to acknowledge the need for cross-departmental teamwork, driven by the demand for expertise in areas such as cloud computing. This perspective underscores the adaptability and teamwork within the workplace, illustrating the fact that interdepartmental collaboration is crucial for successfully completing projects: "However, in some cases, collaboration with people from other departments is necessary, especially when it comes to certain technologies, such as cloud technologies, for which experts from other departments are available" (I1).

3.2.6   Team's Autonomy Degree

The significance of a team within an embedded technology department is clear in various situations throughout the organisation, showcasing its vital role in the development processes. Employees highlight the team's integration into the broader development group and underline some unique functions that are critical to the overall framework. Moreover, referencing the team's contributions to client projects underscores their external duties and places a focus on client needs. The discussion about utilising different tools suggests a level of adaptability and flexibility in accomplishing development tasks, underlining the team's expertise in employing various tools for the implementation of the project: "But the role of the team is to develop, so we are part of the development group of this embedded technology department and we have, I don't know exactly how many roles belong to this development, and we contribute to client and project development activities, mainly with various tools" (I28).

The role of an HR department within an organisation is often discussed in various contexts. Acting as a third-party entity, the department intentionally adopts a neutral position and avoids becoming emotionally involved in the daily operations of delivery teams. This stated independence from delivery processes involves clearly defining roles and emphasising accountability. The phrase "a degree of internal independence" suggests a balanced approach, allowing for both autonomy and potential collaboration. Overall, this representation indicates a conscious effort to establish the impartiality of the HR division as an entity within the corporate framework: "Well, as I said, we are a human resources department. Therefore, we try to be a sort of independent viewpoint. In order not to get emotionally involved in everything that happens in the delivery departments, we try to be objective for the department. We work independently of the delivery processes and procedures. So, we have a certain degree of internal independence here" (I17).

Further opinions discuss the company's organisational dynamics and highlight the essential link between team productivity and the relevance of each department. They suggest a mutually beneficial relationship between a department's vitality and the effectiveness of its staff. The team approaching maturity indicates a growth process, demonstrating a greater level of self-reliance and independence in completing tasks effectively. Overall, the description points to an advancement within the organisational structure, reinforcing the cohesion and autonomy of teams as they progress within their specific areas. "I would say that when we talk about a company with so many departments and such a broad objective, I couldn't say for sure, but in my department, definitely. So, if the department is an essential one, then yes, the team is also efficient, the answer is related. And the team itself, I would say it is practically at the point of reaching maturity, so they are self-sufficient and quite independent in their tasks" (I24).

3.3 Influencing Factor Number 3: Stability (Organisational (in)Stability and (Dis)Continuity)

This topic refers to discussions taking place within the organisation, specifically analysing how internal changes affect a particular group, likely in Romania. Some staff members perceive the complexity of the issue, noting that it extends beyond the purpose of a single department. The reference to a dynamic organisational environment refers to the fact that both shifts within the company and the broader group are at play. While some employees believe that factors of high-level politics can influence local operations and maybe perhaps cause instability, others seem somewhat disconnected from these transformations. Adaptability in response to potential changes is essential when it comes to future uncertainty and its implications for various aspects of the workplace: "So, this is one aspect, but it is explained very succinctly, on a very small scale, because it is a very broad discussion, which we will not complete this semester. It also comes from within the company because, in terms of the company itself and the group we are part of, changes are taking place and, of course, this will have an impact and will probably cause instability for us, for DATA-CO in Romania, from my point of view, because, to be honest, I am not that familiar with high-level policy within DATA-CO or globally, but some aspects reach us and a certain impact can be seen in the organisation, let's say, in the form of instability. Because we are not sure what will happen regarding various aspects of our workplace" (I11).

Our study describes the difficulties presented by a complex communication structure within the organisation, especially with discontinuity and instability. In order to establish a shared hierarchical understanding, our study points out the difficulties in negotiating across various management levels. Despite active participation in meetings and requests for updates, there has been a lack of crucial information, resulting in serious consequences. Specifically, a considerable amount of time and effort will be required to rectify the recent work that has been invalidated. This situation demonstrates the importance of clear communication channels and the potential fallout from not sharing vital information promptly and thoroughly within the organisation:

"Often, there are too many levels of communication, with two managers going to other managers, who then go to other managers. Just yesterday, I found out that a colleague and I are at almost the same level, with the same hierarchy of managers, but different horizontally and vertically. And we both found out that we hadn't been informed about something very important for our work. Basically, my work from the last two weeks has been cancelled because I didn't have the right information. So now I have to redo all the contracts, all the calculations, and everything else. For me personally, it's very time-consuming and a lot of effort not to be informed about something. And even though I participated in all the calls, even though I insisted on this, it's something that has only come up now" (I25).

The current workforce perceives their environment as stable, but they also recognise potential volatility due to significant changes in team composition. Based on previous experiences with the organisation, some employees remembered the frequent changes in team managers, which were initially perceived as a sign of instability. The years 2020 and 2021 are referenced, providing context for the situation. People's interpretations differ in viewpoints, which is a sign that these changes may not have been perceived as unstable at the time. This statement offers a thoughtful assessment of how employees' views on stability and instability have evolved over time, influenced by their previous workplace experiences: "This is my perception at this moment of stability, where instability could arise with major fluctuations, and, in the case of teams, rapid changes in leadership. We have had this experience before in the company, with people frequently leaving the organisation, and I perceived this at the time as a source of instability, but I am referring now to 2020 or 2021. So that was my perception at the time. I did not perceive it as instability" (I26).

A strong connection has been identified within the corporation between organisational stability and levels of transparency. Our research suggests that insufficient transparency leads to instability. On the other side, increased transparency facilitates the creation of precise schedules for the forthcoming months or years, acting as a guide for future occurrences. The importance of transparency in sustaining stability within the organisational structure is highlighted by its role as a key factor in planning and forecasting: "Normally, instability comes from transparency. If there is greater transparency, you can have a plan for the next year, for the next month, and you know how things should unfold in the future, next month or next year or something like that" (I7).

Sometimes, a possible challenge in the workplace could be that people find themselves unprepared for the tasks assigned to them. This deficiency in preparation can hinder or obstruct the workflow. It's important to acknowledge that there are times when teammates or coworkers may not have the necessary skills or background for the tasks assigned to them. In such situations, collaboration and support become crucial. It is essential to acknowledge that the time needed to support less experienced colleagues may be longer than expected. This dynamic highlights the necessity of addressing skill deficiencies and cultivating a supportive atmosphere to reduce the likelihood of workflow disruptions. Additionally, increased transparency allows for the development of clear plans for the upcoming months or years, providing a useful roadmap: "Perhaps sometimes people are not very well prepared for the work they have to do and perhaps they need help. That is when disruptions or discontinuities can occur. Yes, sometimes we have colleagues who are members of the team and who do not have much experience, do not have the necessary skills for the work they do. Yes, when that happens, we have to help them, and, you know, the time you spend on something becomes longer than you estimated or expected, or something like that" (I11).

Even if any potential for discontinuities is appreciated, their impact is mitigated by the diversity within the organisational portfolio. The environment is lively, thanks to a variety of clients and ongoing opportunities. This vibrancy increases organisational performance as it facilitates quick responses. Additionally, the adaptability of the organisational framework is confirmed by its capacity to shift personnel across different tasks. This indicates that the intrinsic dynamic of the organisational structure facilitates proactive problem-solving and resource reallocation, ensuring an adaptable and flexible operational model when facing expected challenges: "So, this can be seen as a discontinuity, but in most cases, because we have several clients in our portfolio and also opportunities every time, it is very dynamic, we can easily find solutions and distribute, redistribute people within another project" (I28).

3.3.1 (In)stability and (Dis)continuity in Functional/ Departmental Teams

A few remarks about stability and continuity in functional teams underline the differences between two departments: the partner management unit and the staffing and recruitment department. The partner management unit is highly regarded by the staff for its professionalism, especially in terms of their consistent communication, logical procedures and reliable responses. In contrast to relationships with other departments which are sometimes challenging, this positive dynamic is notably distinct: "I think one of the best examples I can give is the recruitment and selection department. Alongside this is the department that deals with the partners who work for us. I think this is an example of professionalism, of how things should be done professionally, of the interaction between employees, of their way of working, their constant, normal reactions, workflow, continuity, inexistence of problems, as you would say, so for me it is always something that... when I think about it, I don't have a negative feeling about it, I don't feel that the situation is serious, as is sometimes the case with other departments, where, even before sending an email, I know that I won't get a reply in time, but it's something very good and it has improved a lot in the last 12-15 months thanks to the person who took over the position and the manager, who is doing a very good job of handling this part, and I think that this aspect of behaviour and organisation can lead to the continuation and maintenance of a good, calmer, and more efficient workplace. Okay, so staffing and recruitment, not HR, HR handles internal personnel management" (I25).

The structure of larger teams often needs to adapt because of the industry dynamics in which the organisation operates. The study stresses the unpredictability of their work environment by presenting examples where, over a span of six months, nearly half of a team faces notable changes due to employee turnover and the onboarding of new members. This trend could extend beyond single initiatives and potentially occur inside department structures. The presence of a cyclical pattern of staff changes is recommended, resulting from the frequent team reconfiguration. This example reveals the challenges generated by high employee turnover rates and the necessity for organisational flexibility to effectively manage the evolving team structures: "Due to the field we work in, larger teams are constantly changing. For example, I have worked on projects where, in half a year, half the team changed, half the people quit and were replaced. I assume this also happens within departments, where people quit and others have to take their place very often" (I22).

A clear example of discontinuity occurs when a subgroup within an organisation announces upcoming changes to structures, roles or the organisation itself. The speaker notes that although communication regarding the impact of these changes on specific areas may be unclear, the anticipation of possible links and shifts within the group can lead to a sense of discontinuity. The employer acknowledges the arbitrary nature of these changes, noting that the actual transitions may not align with individuals' perceptions of how they will impact their specific roles. This proves the psychological dimension of managing organisational changes and the volatility that can arise from assumptions about how broader changes will influence specific areas within the organisation: "Another element of discontinuity would be when the group decides or announces that it will change certain structures, certain roles, certain organisations, and so on. This can be an element of discontinuity, not necessarily because you are directly informed that your area will be affected or changed, but because the connections you establish may be altered, within the group, having an impact on my area, but this is only an assumption; it may not actually influence us" (I26).

3.3.2 (In)stability and (Dis)continuity in Social and People Structures Overall

Employees identify sources of continuity within the broader organisational framework, reinforcing the essential roles that openness and shared values play. One of the key elements supporting organisational continuity is transparency. It is also highlighted that in order to thrive continuity, individual values must align with the organisation's values. Our research indicates that a company cultivates a sense of continuity when it actively seeks to understand and align with the values of its workforce. Moreover, the alignment of an individual's personal values with the organisational structure is a crucial factor in their engagement with the business. From this point of view, openness, shared values and organisational continuity are interconnected, with mutual understanding and alignment in values contributing positively to the overall environment: "There are sources of continuity in general and within the organisation in particular, and I believe that the sources of continuity are transparency and, how can I put it, finding my values within the company, you know, and yes, the fact that we have common values, human resources and the organisation, I believe that common values are the human resources and the organisation and they are sources of continuity, and as much as the organisation does something to establish the values that human resources have, it will be able to ensure continuity, and as much as human resources find themselves in terms of their own values within the organisation, they will continue to be part of the organisation" (I14).

Observable evidence of possible instability is the frequent turnover that happens when several employees leave, leading to an influx of new, significantly younger recruits. A catalyst for instability in the workforce is represented by younger generations, prompting the need for different strategies and management approaches. The generational gap requires the development of new ideas and tactics, hence resulting in a revitalised perception of disruption and unpredictability inside the organisational structure. This depiction underscores the challenges of adapting to shifts in the workforce and the dynamic nature of organisational stability while adjusting to ongoing staff transitions: "Another example would be that many colleagues left and then we had many new colleagues, new employees, people who joined the team, but they were very young. And that is again an unstable situation because usually young people from other generations need to be treated differently, as you must come up with new ideas and strategies. And that creates instability and disruption again. And it's a bit difficult" (I3).

3.3.3 Client Perceptions About Company's (In)stability and (Dis)continuity and the Influence of the Labour Market

Possible interruptions are seen as inputs that may arise from internal concerns or client escalations. However, these do not seem to create long-term disruptions. Instead, the company has a responsive system where individuals can express their concerns, leading to immediate response from the Competence Centre Manager or the Delivery Manager. This proactive approach treats the initial issue as a temporary event within a broader context, facilitating a quick solution. The focus is on the company's capacity to manage and mitigate disruptions to prevent them from evolving into extended periods of uncertainty: "These can be entries, meaning they can have the same importance and represent an escalation from a client. It's not a long-term disruption, but, as you know, people raise their hands and then the delivery manager comes and helps them or the Competence Centre Manager, depending on the issue. So, it starts as continuity, but it doesn't last as a disruption" (I23).

The company has managed to maintain its client base over time, even if there were changes in Europe's IT&C sector. Despite facing some uncertainty in recent years, it has been fortunate to avoid significant disruptions, showcasing its resilience in keeping client relationships stable: "We haven't lost many clients over the years. I know there has been some instability in the IT&C market, even in Europe. But I don't think we've been lucky to not face that at a high level in the last two years" (I17). The job market seems to be an intense competition, companies providing many opportunities in terms of positions and remuneration. Many individuals perceive their career opportunities as a game, often linking it to poker. The statement above describes a personal experience from the author's activity within a technical team, highlighting that more than half of the forty members transitioned to different roles throughout their tenure. This remark highlights the changing and competitive landscape of the professional world where individuals strategically manage their career paths in the current job market: "I think there are so many options in the professional world, in terms of jobs and salaries, that there is competition, I think, between jobs, that is, between what organisations and companies offer as jobs. And that's why I've noticed that so many people treat work as a kind of game. I could call it the poker game. I was part of a technical team for a year and a half before I ended up on the bench. It was a team of about 40 people. More than half of them changed jobs over time" (I14).

3.4 Influencing Factor Number 4: Closure

3.4.1 Sense of Belonging

According to our research, some employees who have worked for the company for 14 years have developed a strong sense of attachment and belonging. This prolonged tenure has resulted in a robust emotional bond, underscoring the importance of their past association with the organisation in cultivating this bond: "I have been with the company for 14 years. Therefore, I could say I feel a very strong sense of belonging to the company" (I23).

A decrease in emotional attachment and a sense of belonging is a major factor in employee attrition inside the company, according to other discussions. As these sentiments fade, employee-organisation relationships shift towards more impersonal and business-oriented interactions, becoming more transactional: "So, I would say that the biggest impact and also one of the main causes of people leaving the company was that the sense of belonging and attachment diminished, and the relationship became more transactional" (I23).

Even if someone leaving a team or organisation could leave a gap, everyone believes that anyone can take their place, including the departing individual. By claiming that they do not consider themselves especially significant members of the team or organisation, some employees manifest an understanding of their replaceability: "I think leaving a group or a certain organisation could leave a void, a small empty space there. But everyone is replaceable. Well, I don't feel like I'm an important person in the team or in the organisation" (I14).

Other feedback shows that a major cause of the organisation's high employee turnover rate is given by the fact that staff members feel a stronger connection to the client than to the company. This also implies the idea that having strong client relationships could be a major factor in employee attrition: "Because many people are leaving the company. And the feedback is that they seem more connected to the client than to DATA-CO (I5)".

3.4.2 Self-identification as an Employee

Employee values the freedom to approach their work in a manner that suits them best. Their alignment with the company's values and the flexibility in their roles foster a strong sense of belonging within the organisation. This connection and comfort are opposed to a previous job where strict rules dictated how they performed their tasks. As significant changes influence the organisation, employees are grateful for the opportunity to share their creativity and innovative ideas. They perceive this as a fantastic platform where they can exchange creative concepts and strategies: "So, for me, it's very important to have the freedom to do my job the way I think is right. Based on these values, I feel that I belong to this company. Or even more than that. Yes, I identify myself as an employee because I feel very comfortable in the company I work for, I don't have this limitation because the rules are very strict. For example, you can't do something that's not related to your tasks. If you have ideas, I don't know, I think they're related to your tasks, and you can't do more. And I think it's not valuable for an employee to just do their tasks, finish them, and close their laptop, maybe they don't know about the creativity or ideas that come up. It's very valuable to listen and maybe put it into practice. And when a company is undergoing a major transformation, it's a space where you can put a lot of ideas into practice, a lot of new good practices or processes or something like that" (I9).

3.4.3 Self-differentiation from Other Employees in Similar Companies

Many workers feel that their current position is distinctive for a few key reasons. The opportunity to communicate directly to the CEO means that senior management prioritises employee input. This open line of communication is seen as beneficial for their careers. Additionally, employees consider themselves apart by actively engaging in internal initiatives aimed to enhance working conditions and standards for their colleagues. These unique opportunities distinguish them as a different type of employee compared to those in other organisations. While they may not conduct a detailed comparison of workers at other organisations, they consider participation in quality improvement initiatives and open communication to be vital aspects of their current employer: "Well, I am considered different because, in a way, I feel that I can talk directly to the CEO of the company. This means that senior management is very open to discussions with employees. And I find this very positive for my current career in senior management. And I am considered different because I have this opportunity to apply for this type of internal project, with the aim of improving quality and the working environment for employees. Yes, that is why I consider myself different as an employer compared to other companies. I haven't analysed employees in other companies too much, but in a way, from this point of view, I think that's important in this company right now" (I7).

Services provided to different consumers tend to be quite similar when looking at businesses that follow the same model. If an employee decides to switch to another company with a similar strategy, they should expect changes in management and the people they interact with. Particularly regarding the hiring process, our interviews shed light on the clear goals and actions within the current organisation. This familiarity with ongoing activities and involvement in hiring gives people the impression that the current firm is actively involved in multiple facets of its operations. Even though they acknowledge it may not be perfect, they strongly believe that finding another company that offers significantly more than theirs is a challenge: "Yes, if I were to think of similar companies as a business model, because ultimately, we offer services to different clients, I would say yes. Honestly, I think if I changed companies now, I would more or less benefit from the same things. I mean, it would be the same business model. So, if I went to another company with the same business model, of course the management would be different, the people I interact with would be different. But I can see initiatives here. Thus, I know what to expect, I know how to make connections. Of course, it's not perfect, but I see action. I mean, I see what's happening. And I know because I'm involved, as I said, in the recruitment process. So, I know what's going on when I'm working, I know what our companies do. I probably wouldn't find a company that does more than we do" (I28).

Compared to friends at other companies, working in this organisation offers a distinctive chance for differentiation. The speaker emphasises this by pointing out how their friends' roles have remained unchanged for the past decade, while they have different roles within the company.

Throughout the years, the company has played a crucial role in helping them shape their career journey. Their diverse responsibilities and the organisation's support in fostering their professional growth distinguish them from peers who have stayed in the same roles for a long period: "Working for DATA-CO allows me to differentiate myself from others because I have friends who work for other companies and, for example, they do the same thing. They have been doing the same thing for 10 years. Not me, I have changed roles. I have changed many roles over the years, and the company has helped me find my place in the organisation" (I4).

Even when individuals hold a positive view of their current employer, our interviews indicate that there are other companies in the same sector that are viewed with even more admiration and esteem. This reflects a sense of modesty, as they do not perceive themselves as particularly important or valued within their organisation. Their self-assessment is represented by how they measure up against other companies. In essence, their self-worth is shaped by the benchmark set by the firm they are comparing themselves to: "But there are other companies that are even more respected and appreciated. And, yes, in that case, maybe I don't consider myself important, powerful, or appreciated. So, it depends on the company I'm comparing myself to" (I6).

CHAPTER 4

Navigating the Future: Insights and Adaptations in Organisational Landscape

Abstract The future of work is characterised by a shift towards hybrid and remote models, where the organisational dynamics is being more and more influenced by technology, social capital and the necessity for an adaptive leadership style in the IT&C sector. This chapter explores the way in which the future of work, marked by the widespread adoption of remote work and digital transformations, influences organisational social capital (OSC) and involves a profound rethinking of managerial practices. Given the increased mobility, the need for flexibility and diversification of employee expectations, organisations are called to adapt sustainable and innovative strategies for cohesion, retention and collaboration.

Among the identified challenges we note a reduced number of informal interactions, a decrease in the sense of belonging and communication difficulties in the virtual environment. As an answer, there are managerial recommendations proposed, which are concentrated on the development of an empathic and results-oriented leadership style, the promotion of an organisational culture adapted to hybrid work, the encouragement of authentic interactions and the valorisation of human relations in a digital context. Therefore, this chapter underlines the importance of a balance between technology and human interaction in order to support social and organisational changes and to create a sustainable work climate in the post-pandemic era.

Keywords Future work scenarios · Managerial recommendations

© The Author(s), under exclusive license to Springer Nature Switzerland AG 2025
D. Ivana et al., *The Dynamics of Social Capital in Romania's IT&C Sector*, https://doi.org/10.1007/978-3-032-01874-8_4

4.1 Future Work Scenarios

According to Dries, Luyckx and Rogiers (2023) even though the topic of the future of work is "booming", empirical study has been rather uncommon up to this point. We think the reason for this is clear: since the future cannot yet be observed, it is difficult to imagine how to gather scientific data about it (Augustine et al., 2019). Therefore, most of the current research on the future of work can be divided into two categories: the first examines how new technologies are being implemented and used in the workplace today, and the second tries to forecast the nature of work in future using macroeconomic labour market indicators.

Studies in the literature that examine topics like gig work, telework, eHRM, new organisational structures, and job reshaping (Santana & Cobo 2020) reveal patterns of technology use that are novel now but are anticipated to become standard in future.

In this section, employees described their perception of possible future work scenarios and their influence on the creation of Organisational Social Capital (OSC) versus its unrealistic nature in building OSC. The transformations given by the future of work force companies to rethink the way they build human relations, coordinate teams and cultivate their social capital. Remote work, accelerated digitalisation and diversified expectations require constant adaptation of traditional management tools.

In a world where hybrid collaboration, and remote and distributed teams become the rule, managers need a more flexible people approach, led by trust, autonomy and effective communication. More than streamlining operations, this means businesses need to be proactive in developing genuine relationships in a culture that promotes stability, engagement and professional development of employees.

The main code, *future work scenarios*, posits the preference of employees to continue the hybrid work model that was fostered within the last two years prior to the interviews: "Hence, I would say that work will remain wherever it is. And if we adapt to people's flexibility" (I23). Going back to the pre-pandemic situation is seen as the least plausible. Work from home or work from anywhere would be preferable: "Yes. I see this as a continuation of working from anywhere (I1), as well as renting attractive locations outside the office where meetings and workshops could take place". Some interviewees also mention that employees cannot be forced to return to the office or be required to be present for several days, so employees will decide based on their own interests, not in the interest of the organisation: "And, as a result, the employee will obviously make a decision in their own interest and choose what is best for them, not what is best for the organisation" (I14).

Other employees state that this choice depends upon the maturity of each team and the type of work it most suited along the way, while other think that it depends on the task at hand, hence programmers and developers are used to and prefer a work–from-home or work-from-anywhere status quo, as well for the majority of work arrangements, an on the site presence being necessary only when the task is important to be carried out at client premises: "You can request physical presence whenever necessary and justified, such as being present at the office for a meeting or at the client's premises, and this is non-negotiable when it is important, but also when it is not necessary and it is more efficient for programmers, developers, or other specific roles to work from wherever they need to and feel most comfortable, so that they can complete their tasks more quickly. This makes sense" (I6). Regarding reaching common goals, fostering shared identity or assuring a common work culture, interviewees are unsure of the role of hybrid work.

Regarding the possibility of returning to a pre-pandemic work arrangement, almost all interviewees consider it unrealistic. Only one employee states that: "The best scenario is the first one, a return to the pandemic situation" (I27). The remainder of the employees interviewed feel that going back to the pre-pandemic situation is undesirable and would not be accepted by employees if the company tried to impose it. Arguments that ground this statement relate to the waste of time going to and from the office, effects on health, pollution, stress and also, possible depressions: [...] "Don't go back to the office. All you're doing is polluting. You're creating stressful situations, people are getting depressed, because there are scientific studies that show that if you spend more than 20 minutes in traffic, you can become depressed. Or you can get a serious [illness], and if you become depressed, you can have serious health problems. So, it's not healthy, either for our bodies or our minds, to spend a lot of time in traffic. Therefore, I would say that would be the worst-case scenario, going back to full-time office work" (I4). Other employees state that they would hand in their resignation if the company forced them to return to the offices in person, every day. Other employees noted that the company already downsized by reducing the number of rented office places, hence, a 100% return to the offices would be unrealistic. Also, because other companies in the same industry have shifted to this hybrid model, this additional pressure would hold back the company in question from forcing a full in-person model.

Regarding continuing work from anywhere, we can see that employees appreciate this: "So, work from anywhere with the help of workshops. Again, if teams have the freedom to choose when and, if necessary, where to meet (I10)" but in a form that requires maximum one meeting per month in person, or not even that: "So, continuing to work from anywhere, with regular weekly meetings or meetings at the office, well, working from anywhere seems like a good idea to me. But once a week, to make this mandatory, will be difficult and will have a rather negative impact on stability. Perhaps also on interest. Working from anywhere with quarterly workshops and attractive locations could work, because not only does it allow work, but it also enhances the sense of belonging, the sense of stability, and improves people's experience. As long as it's not mandatory" (I10). There are interviewees who think that being present in person is something that other employees wish: "Well, that's something we're trying to do, at least I am in the team. I do it at least once every three months. We organise a meeting outside the working hours. But again, I have to push for it more and more, because I don't want to give up so easily, because, as I said, there are some people who are more inclined to get involved in these activities" (I28) and employees who think that spending time and sharing experiences that enhance social activities is important to be fulfilled by being present in person at the workplace: "Going to the office has an element of surprise, an element of celebration, something special about it. So, I don't go there just to spend a boring day at work. No, I don't do that. And if I have the opportunity to choose between spending precious time with the team, in an attractive place, working and discussing and, you know, satisfying that little need for social interaction, I will do it" (I14). Also, other employees would like to spend the few meetings in person within a workshop that takes place in another location than the office, mainly because another environment would boost the maximisation of OSC: "Yes, it would be useful to have three such workshops in different attractive locations. It might be interesting. […]" (I11), or alternative networking methods, such as after work gatherings, but other employees state that employees who work from home are not necessarily likely to be present: "The problem is that colleagues do not attend these events because, if they work from home, they do not see a reason or one strong enough to attend these events after work" (I21). Still, there are employees who think that attending the workplace in person is marked by several nuisances such as: "[…] Working in an open space, everyone participates in conference calls, you can't concentrate, everyone is talking loudly. There is movement, traffic outside, a lot of noise that distracts you from concentrating" (I2). Another employee sees this alternative as being definitely one that contributes towards maximising OSC: "So, I choose this regularly because it also increases social capital. I am referring to networking and, yes, thirdly, to the three- to four-day workshops in various attractive locations" (I18). Another employee thinks that this choice depends on project's location, team members' seniority and the project at hand, because it would be important for younger employees or new joiners to have a connection with team members: "Yes, I think that's the best solution, but it also depends on the team's project, whether they are in the same location or not, and how long the employees have been with the company. Because at the beginning, you need someone to help you" (I13). Also, management representatives state that there is a plan of continuing the hybrid work model with workshops in different attractive locations, also because employees have expressed this wish: "We conducted several interviews with our colleagues to find out what benefits they would like to have and what kind of interaction we could offer each other. Most voted for the idea of having a different location, not our buildings in big cities, but like a camp, let's say, in a beautiful place in the countryside" (I33).

However, there are few employees who think that continuing work-from-anywhere model with regular in-person, e.g. once a week, meetings at the organisation, would not suit the maximisation of OSC: "[…] Once a week or meetings within the organisation would be possible, but I wouldn't count on it too much [...] Yes, I don't think this will really contribute or influence the social capital of the organisation very much, because these types of three- or four-day meetings, including a workshop, will only bring together people from within the department, but you won't feel connected to the company" (I28). Another employee thinks that people are less efficient while working from home, not wanting to switch back, because they feel that working remote would be the easiest solution, but one that lacks interaction: "But if we try to push ourselves and get there within a certain time frame, social interaction would increase, and our well-being and mental state would improve in a positive way. Okay. So, people just need to be there, even if they don't see the benefits right away, in a few months they will see the benefits, that's my opinion. And I think that works for me" (I20). Finally, one statement referring to the actual legal possibilities to assure working agreements and arrangements within the company states the (im)possible: "It is not possible to work from anywhere, as the law does not allow this. As a company, you must pay certain taxes for employees who work from Germany or another country. So, the idea of working from anywhere is just a concept that does not apply in reality" (9).

In relation to a hybrid model with 2 days in office, 3 days' work from anywhere or 3 days in office, 2 days' work from anywhere, employees feel that this model should be adopted because there are projects that require specific tasks or equipment whereas others think that this might lead to enhancing social capital "Perhaps a hybrid model, to be here more often and because, being here more often, you interact with other people in some way and see other events that are happening more and more often. I think this hybrid model would bring in more capital, but I'm not so sure it can be achieved" (I28). Also, it is the opinion of other employees that such condition of also being present in person should not be forced but understood by the employees: "[...] We need to convey to them why it makes sense to be in the office, why, to a certain extent, we need to be in the office, and we need to repeat this and present it in multiple ways so that people understand". Still, among other options, employees state "I think everyone stands to gain from the hybrid model. In the long term. Maybe I'm wrong, I have no idea. But so far, the hybrid model is the best solution for everyone" (I6). However, one employee thinks that this hybrid model might vanish in time, as possible paradigm shifts might emerge within this industry: "I would prefer the hybrid model, as I mentioned, with three days working in the office and two at home, but I am not entirely sure that people would want that. Because sometimes certain behavioural changes occur after a pandemic. People do not want to come to the office; perhaps they have other jobs or other projects. They are very anxious. So, from my point of view, it's very, very difficult to change their behaviour. So, I don't think I know how that could happen. Even if I see that it's the best model. Most likely, we'll continue like this until, I don't know, there's a crisis in the industry and we won't be able to be so picky anymore" (I20).

Also, another employee sheds light upon another aftermath effect: "I also believe that a hybrid model, with two days in the office and three days working from home or something similar, is not something that most people would want. And that third option seems most likely to me, because I know people who have decided to move out of the big cities where [company name] or other companies are based and are moving either back to their hometowns or to smaller towns where housing is much more affordable and where the money they earn goes further. And for that, a model where you have to return to the city at least once a week is not feasible, and these people have decided that now that they can find a job that is not tied to a physical location or a geographical place, they prefer to look for a geographical place to live and then choose their job based on that decision" (I22).

4.2 Future Possibilities

Moving on to the main code future possibilities, with respect to improving existing interactive portals, only two interviewees state that their improvement would not be necessary, hence employees do not use them, or their existence would not improve life significantly: "No, no. I think I'm fine. I think there's a... I don't think it might improve or change your life in any extraordinary way" (I25). The rest of the interviewees think that improving the existing portals, not necessarily developing new ones, would rather be beneficial, hence they are working, and should only be adapted to meet new requirements of new generations. The use of existing portals has shown to engage employees in striving to reach goals for the company, as a community: "[…] where there is a common goal to run or practice sports, and companies have a certain set of personal goals with certain points, and we have seen many people who have signed up and run and cycled to raise the company's level, so the portals are helpful. We also think that it's something new in the community, something that's been implemented recently. People interact through the portals because it's something we're used to from apps on our phones. We like interacting that way. It's easy and doesn't cause anxiety" (I20). Overall, we can notice an agreement upon improving the existing portals, the statement above and others as well, pointing out the value thereof.

Developing new interactive portals is favoured by most interviewees "I think we should develop new interactive portals. This topic is also on our agenda" (I19), and there is only one interviewee who thinks that such development would not be necessary: "Seriously, I think it's enough. Okay" (I11). The contribution of their development is mainly noted within enhancing employee's involvement and communication. Portals are also seen as highly useful tools, though their effectiveness depends on how they are implemented. In this matter, one interviewee states that if portals are interactive and employees also can contribute towards designing them, they would be successful. Also, enhancing digitalisation of information and actively contributing towards it is seen as being a trend setter on behalf of the company. Adding gamification to this tool is seen as positive. In the same line of thought, this is seen as an opportunity, and if portals are developed correctly and in an attractive way, they would be a strength, hence companies would then have lesser nuisance. Portal's redesign is seen as a necessity, because according to some interviewees, portals haven't been developed since they were initially designed.

Regarding the adoption and use of metaverse as a measure that might influence Organisational Social Capital, most of the interviewees would not favour its implementation: "We had those metaverses. No, definitely not, I don't think so. I don't believe in the metaverse. Personally, I don't believe in it" (I1). The reasons include the wish to spend less time using technology, thus having more time for outdoor activity, and the need to ensure a clear delimitation between activities that are of professional versus personal nature. While some interviewees think that metaverse might be somehow beneficial for professional purposes, they would completely exclude any involvement of family members. Some interviewees that view metaverse as a possible, future new way, think of it as being a part of an AI trend and a tool of online, written communication, that would ease feeling comfortable in relation to others. On behalf of the management team, there are statements that metaverse is already being used as an onboarding tool within another branch of the company, while using avatars for interaction. But there are several interviewees who think that metaverse would be suitable only for a younger generation. Still, there are interviewees, representatives of the younger generation that currently use technology, who would not favour metaverse, because this would mean additional technology and gears that must be integrated in one's daily life. Other employees would simply just favour in-person interactions and others think that metaverse would just foster further isolation and would not have an impact in building up social capital: "I mean, metaverse may be an interesting concept, but I think it will isolate people even more. I don't think metaverse could be a solution for improving social capital" (I28). Further, one employee addresses the ethical aspect of integrating metaverse if its use would be in a conflictual situation with own beliefs and values. Overall, it is remarkable that metaverse is approached with caution.

Concerning the addition of the following features/elements to the existing/new interactive portals such as emotional connection, interviewees view emotional connection as being important, but mainly accomplished through coaching of managers, rather than through interactive portals. Emotional connection would in this sense be effective, only if it improves the connection between managers and their colleagues. Other interviewees feel that there already is enough emotional involvement whereas others prefer to work remote and do not feel the need for additional emotional bond. Others feel that managers should be more empathetic, not more emotional, whereas one other employee states that being emotional would enable bonding but would also have down sided effects, if it gets misused: "If we manage to create an emotional connection with our colleagues, of course, this can be very beneficial and helpful. But it will also open doors for exploitation. Personally, I wouldn't like that. I like to establish an emotional connection with my colleagues because it helps us build trust. I don't think I would be so open to building this emotional connection with my manager, of course, because I've known them for a long time. But with someone new to the company, because I never want to open the door that can be used to exploit my feelings" (I4).

Another interviewee states that gathering up a kind of statistic through an interactive portal would be beneficial for the company: "I know there is talk about creating this interactive portal or something that is not exactly a social network, but a way in which, with a single click, you can express your feelings on that particular day. And maybe it is clearer for the company to see statistics about what is happening or what the current emotional state is, or not even emotional, the state of that employee who wants to say, 'Okay, I'm sad or upset about these things'" (I15).

Refining manager roles is also seen as an initiative meant to enhance social capital: "[…] Perhaps we should rethink and redefine the role of the manager. I believe this will help us develop organisational social capital in the future, to have a managerial role based on and created around the needs of our colleagues, and this manager must be adaptable, flexible, wear, I don't know, different masks, if I may say so, and different clothes, depending on the person in front of them, know their colleagues very well, and then establish an emotional connection based on what they need" (I3). Thus, managers need to be more people oriented, develop more people skills and personal interactions should be prioritised, not interactive portals, hence these would help only on the short run, not on the long run. Still, another employee thinks that some initiatives of being part of the company's community and social initiatives which are clearly meant for bonding are kind of part of the deal. Also, more focus should be on authentic relationships towards a growth mindset.

For some interviewees, gamification is seen as a method to engage employees within competition and challenges and thus reward them, hence it will bring people together, but it might also have negative consequences. However, other employees think that gamification should be adapted to the different generations working in the company, because they have different needs and expectations. We also note that these gamified systems are already implemented within branches of this company within other countries but are not currently implemented in Romania. Another employee thinks that gamification might make tasks and projects more interesting, and attractive.

For other interviewees, gamification is seen as a method to engage employees within competition and challenges and thus reward them, hence it will bring people together, but it might also have negative consequences such as: "This gamification thing always offers rewards, and I don't think we should do that even for people in the IT&C sector, for the period in which gamification could be used, but we have to understand that not all results require a reward. I mean, you always ask for a reward, and then we talk a lot about the size of the reward for the work done, for completing tasks, and so on" (I8). Another possible downside would be the development of enthusiasm in the beginning of such an activity, enthusiasm that has proven to fade away over time: "People are enthusiastic at first, but when something has to happen, many of them give up or don't want to continue, so, in theory, everyone wants this social capital to improve. I understand that, but the problem or discontinuity arises when things happen. The first problem is at the company level, where we may not have the exact methods to apply. And second, I think there is this anxiety that we all feel after these pandemics" (I20).

Nevertheless, other employees think that gamification should be adapted to the different generations working in the company, because they have different needs and expectations. We also note that these gamified systems are already implemented within branches of this company within other countries but are not currently implemented in Romania. Another employee thinks that gamification might make tasks and projects more interesting and attractive. Another interviewee is concerned that people will be more focused on the result, rather than on the process. Gamification is also seen as a method towards personnel retention: "Well, money talks. And that's, I think, the most important thing, except that we don't think about money. It's more something we have to do for the development of our colleagues, because everyone has goals. So, I know that to improve stability or continuity, we should probably add gamification" (I4). Also, gamification would create a sense of belonging among employees: "The feeling that you are part of something larger" (I24).

In matters of improving stability/continuity/retention in personnel overall and its influence on Organisational Social Capital, we can notice consensus among the interviewees: "[…] I believe that improving staff stability and continuity in general would be a good way to develop Organisational Social Capital. Okay" (I25). According to one of the managers, social initiatives where employees exchange experiences regarding projects are already happening, and these would bring stability and retention in the long run. Also, one-on-one discussions have taken place, like a stay interview regarding the needs of employees, mainly within the People Experience initiative, that focuses on personal retention. However, social initiatives are unable to offer competitive wages. This is seen as the biggest challenge, hence other social initiatives are already happening: "No, they also receive a salary, not just that, they should receive, I mean not just portals, interactive portals and gamification or discussions with someone, but also material incentives, because we all work to achieve the company's financial goals, only that, and, at some point, they should be more competitive in this regard, in this matter" (I6). As a general vibe, the organisation is bound to invest in the continuous and further development of OSC.

Regarding other possible ways that might influence OSC, interviewees view virtual communication platforms as being important, but also expand the company's network to other cities, thus welcoming new employees. An agile mindset and agile reactions should also be fostered, and establishing a new, own identity, different from competitors. Another employee would appreciate receiving more days off, commensurate with seniority. Hybrid work, enhancing the value of benefits, is also mentioned. Other possible activities that were mentioned are workshops, volunteering activities, hiking and gaming. Also, the value of value is mentioned, hence employees have own values and beliefs that have to be taken into account in order to build OSC: "I have been thinking about other ways to develop organisational social capital in the future, and I mentioned this at one point in our discussion, referring to personal career goals and personal values. I will elaborate on these two aspects a little further here. To the extent that the company understands that employees have their own personal professional goals, the organisation will be able to adapt to the situation because, if the organisation ignores the interests of its employees, they will most likely leave the organisation and move between organisations until they find the place where their goals are best met" (I14).

Also, exchange of experiences within other branches of the companies in other cities are seen as attractive as well as establishing sport teams between these branches. Another employee states that unless such a bonding initiative is compulsory, very few people might attend. Another opinion refers to extending the services within the company. In this respect, the company already has a team of coaches but would also need therapists. Also, regarding the onboarding process, there are interviewees who think this should be adapted to current needs: "[...] Therefore, more communication between departments. That is, if you join the company, as I said, you know that you have a point of stability, even if you change projects or change anything else, or if you already have a trusting relationship with someone [...]" (I13). Also, training regarding skills development was addressed. More feedback from the direct manager regarding own contribution in reaching the company's goals is also mentioned. Another employee remembers that some years ago, the company was smaller and the relationship with the line manager was stronger. Receiving feedback and having an active discussion partner are currently missed.

Improving stability, improving the interactive portals, emotional connection and people skills are the main initiatives meant to be implemented, according to the interviewees.

Overall, the shared consensus is that there should be a mix between hybrid and in-person activities to continue building up OSC.

4.3 Managerial Recommendations

To address these challenges, a set of managerial recommendations must be taken into consideration to redefine leadership styles and strengthen organisational culture in a virtual environment. It is important to form leaders that can manage remote teams, provide constant feedback and emotional support, and create contexts for remote collaboration and networking. At the same time, supporting empathetic and results-oriented leadership contributes to increased commitment and staff retention. Companies can respond to the demands of the future of work and strengthen social capital in the technological-driven era, if initiatives such as developing digital skills, organising virtual events, involving employees' families in online activities or appreciating remote achievements are adopted and consolidated. In the following, we present some practitioners' viewpoints regarding the observed positive and negative effects, the "remote" work model has on organisations from the IT&C sector Table 4.1.

In addition to the *Effects of the "remote" work model*, we identified several difficulties/problems induced by working in a virtual environment:

Table 4.1 Effects of the "remote" work model

Positive	Negative
• access to regional and global talent, where the geographic location could be significantly expanded. • increased efficiency and productivity, achieved through enhanced productivity, allowing employees to better organise their time and work in environments where they feel more comfortable and focused. • decrease in distractions typically encountered in office settings. • decrease in operational costs for workspaces. • companies' ability to quickly adapt to environmental changes, including crisis situations or unforeseen events such as pandemics or natural disasters. • improvement in employee satisfaction and motivation by maintaining a balance between personal and professional life. • decrease of the carbon footprint and environmental impact. • increase in diversity and inclusion among staff, which can bring new perspectives and innovations to the organisation. • migration of operational processes online and digitally leads to increased organisation affinity for innovation, technologies, and new working methods. • following the increased appetite for online interactions from customers, new business strategies and models can be developed.	• diminishing of cohesion and traditional connections among employees. • increase in social isolation and lack of personal interactions, affecting professional development and the sense of belonging to the team. • difficulties in information and communication processes due to possible poor understanding and interpretation of non-verbal cues, vocal tone, facial expressions, and gestures online compared to face-to-face interaction. • absence of informal conversations at the office, leading to the disappearance of rapid information exchange and informal problem-solving. • lack of personal interactions and contact with team colleagues or managerial structures. • monitoring and evaluating employees and their performances remotely can be more challenging than face-to-face. • absence of physical, visual contact may lead to concerns and insecurities regarding productivity and performance, potentially affecting trust and leading to tensions within the organisation. • without countermeasures, maintaining and promoting organisational values and culture can become critical. • decrease in team identification, collective identity, or even overall organisational identification can lead to reduced sense of belonging to the organisation and affect employees' morale and commitment. • organisational culture is often built and maintained through daily interactions and practices in the workplace. Remote work can make it difficult to ensure cultural coherence within the organisation, as employees may have different experiences depending on their location and how they organise their work. • increase in professional identification with the project, technology and end client concurrently with the decrease in allegiance to the employer, negatively impacting workforce stability and leading to an increase in turnover.

- Asynchronous digital communication: In virtual teams, communication primarily occurs through written messages, video calls or other digital means. This can make communication more asynchronous and may require better clarity and documentation.
- Difficulties in reading signals: Without the physical presence of those involved in a conflict, it is more difficult to read subtle signals that may indicate tension or frustration. This can lead to greater uncertainty in interpreting the situation.
- Potential communication delays: Communication in the online environment can involve delays, either due to time zone differences or other technical delays. These delays can prolong the conflict resolution process and amplify tensions.
- Risk of misinterpretation of written messages: Written messages, such as emails or chat messages, are subject to misinterpretation. Written words may not always convey the tone or real intention of a person, which can lead to confusion or more intense conflicts.
- Difficulties in managing emotions: In the online environment, it is more difficult to manage emotions during a conflict. The lack of direct interaction can make individuals feel less accountable for their words and actions, which can escalate the conflict.
- Need for more clarity in communication: Resolving conflicts online often requires clearer and more concise communication to avoid confusion or misinterpretations. It is important to emphasise clarity and formulate messages in a way that minimises ambiguity.
- Potential for conflict escalation: In the online environment, conflicts can escalate more quickly, as some individuals may feel less inhibition in expressing negative opinions or feelings through written messages.
- Quality issues with image or voice, non-use of video cameras, can become additional barriers in managing tense discussions.

Consequently, considering the patterns which emerged from our research, we propose several *pre–/descriptive measures to reduce the negative impact of the "remote" work model* and develop *a virtual organisational culture*:

- Besides implementing online collaboration tools, implement and develop specific remote work techniques, rules and habits.

- Propagation of a management style consistently oriented towards objectives and results rather than supervision or monitoring.
- Development and promotion of virtual leaders with skills in remote team performance management, capable of inspiring, motivating, guiding employees and communicating excellently in the online environment.
- Organisation of training sessions for the management team to develop effective online communication skills, remote performance management, task delegation, balanced allocation in virtual teams, online conflict resolution, etc.
- Promotion of "trust" and "autonomy" as fundamental pillars of a behavioural organisational culture.
- Consistent encouragement of social interactions and professional development remotely, with benefits for employees.
- Increased transparency in decision-making processes by presenting detailed contexts of important decisions affecting individuals' interests.
- Encouragement for employees to share their experiences and challenges and seek help when needed.
- Creation of a best practices guide for remote work and collaboration to ensure coherence and efficiency in the organisation.
- Provision of support, mentorship and resources for remote employees to help them adapt and perform in the new remote work environment.
- Organising online events and activities to promote organisational values and culture, such as training sessions, virtual networking sessions or online volunteering projects.
- Constant promotion and encouragement of organisational values and culture, with remote work being considered a fundamental element in the company's future policy.
- Recognition of efforts and achievements of remote employees is essential for increasing loyalty.
- Regular and constructive feedback regarding successful remote work performances to show employees that their work is valuable and appreciated.
- Provision of opportunities for professional development and continuous learning online, by inviting renowned references. Offer access to resources, courses and training programmes to help employees develop skills and advance in their careers.

- Support in managing stress and maintaining their physical and mental well-being.
- Creating an online company social environment where virtual events, social meetings and online team activities are organised to promote social interaction and connections among employees.
- Encouragement for employees to socialise and connect online and outside strict professional contexts.
- Organisation of virtual events and activities for employees' families, such as online socialising sessions, contests, virtual movie nights or even training sessions for the whole family.
- Allocation of a special day for a "Virtual Family Day", where employees can invite their family members to participate in virtual meetings with their colleagues or explore their projects and achievements. Top managers can present the company's and employees' achievements at such meetings.
- Organisation of virtual competitions or contests in which employees and their families can participate, such as art competitions or photo contests, with prizes and recognition for winners to create an additional incentive for involvement and participation.
- Provision of resources and useful information for employees' families, such as tips for managing work-life balance or resources for children's distance learning.
- Organisation of a special day where employees can bring their family members virtually or physically to the office. Children can attend meetings or participate in fun and interactive activities.
- Open communication with family members by presenting the company's vision, values and social projects online.
- Involvement of employees' families in social or charitable projects organised by the organisation. Promotion of these actions can be done both online and physically.
- Encouragement of employees' family members to provide feedback and suggestions regarding the virtual work environment and how the organisation can better support them.

When speaking about the human resource who is delegated with the above-mentioned measures, we propose a *profile of a virtual leader* who should meet as many characteristics as possible, from the following:

- Builds trust in team members.
- Communicates openly.
- Pays attention to integrating new team members.
- Focuses on results.
- Establishes common team objectives.
- Builds a positive team culture.
- Promotes casual, informal conversations.
- Organises virtual events.
- Makes the process of evaluating online performance more transparent.
- Promotes the use of common collaboration, communication and project management tools.
- Clearly communicates and clarifies objectives and expectations.
- Clearly defines workflows and procedures.
- Holds regular meetings and appointments that are respected and conducted in a disciplined manner.
- Focuses on the team's results rather than hours or attendance.
- Regularly evaluates performance and provides feedback.
- Implements coaching programmes.
- Communicates own availability and preferred communication methods to be reachable by team members.
- Respects working hours, including time zones for international teams.
- Announces meetings and appointments in advance.
- Regularly offers motivational incentives: professional training opportunities, small symbolic gifts, time off, awards, etc.

References

Augustine, G., Soderstrom, S., Milner, D., & Weber, K. (2019). Constructing a distant future: Imaginaries in geoengineering. *Academy of Management Journal*, *62*(6), 1930–1960.

Dries, N., Luyckx, J., & Rogiers, P. (2023). Imagining the (distant) future of work. *Academy of Management Discoveries*, *10*(3). https://doi.org/10.5465/amd.2022.0130

Santana, M., & Cobo, M. J. (2020). What is the future of work? A science mapping analysis. *European Management Journal, 38*, 846–862. https://doi.org/10.1016/j.emj.2020.04.010

CHAPTER 5

Concluding Reflections on the Implications of Social Capital for the Future of Work

Abstract This section illustrates how important it is for organisations to remain open to change and effective communication, both being essential in preserving stability when so much within still changes rapidly around you. This scenario drives employee satisfaction and lowers turnover rates. Although it comes with advantages, like higher productivity and talent pools the size of oceans, it also brings its downsides, such as lack of cohesion and isolation in equal measure. Considering this, the research offers interventions to "humanise" or engage with and improve processes in remote work, including receiving virtual leadership training, developing trust and healthful online culture. In the end, what this research has shown is that adaptability, proactive communication and a complete perspective around employee well-being are building an effective corporate culture.

Keywords Organisational communication · Cross-departmental collaboration. · Organisational resilience. · Organisation belonging. · Retention. · Employee well-being.

The COVID-19 caused various changes in business operations and led to the adoption of innovative methods and resolutions regarding the relationship networks and social support as indicators for employment fulfilment, well-being and performance at the workplace. In this sense, trust represents an important role. Social capital reflects the collective orientation of staff members towards business targets, along with the sense of confidence and relationships they establish with their coworkers (Luthans et al., 2024). Our findings suggest that in general, trust is considered as generalised between coworkers and managers, both vertically and horizontally, and which has strengthened over time, even in a pandemic setting. Moreover, in specific contexts the types of trust that emerged from our data can even be interpreted as resilient and/or dyadic.

Our first research question: *What are the peculiarities of OSC creation in the IT&C sector?*, has in focus the shift to a hybrid model which brought a lot of changes especially in designing a new strategy for cultivating social capital, putting an accent on the challenges and barriers that have emerged in terms of organisational and individual level. Our study confirms that even in hard times, it is relevant to maintain communication, transparency and adaptability when dealing with transitions (Yadav et al., 2024). Despite fluctuations, DATA-CO demonstrated resilience by effectively managing internal challenges and customer relationships, which supports Mahajan et al.'s (2023) theory. The organisation's flexible approach, supportive leadership and collective responsibility contributed to employee satisfaction, job fulfilment and a positive work environment, which is in line with (Mishra & Bharti, 2024) findings. In the same line of thought, it is worth mentioning that DATA-CO's organisational culture places a strong emphasis on meaningful and informal interactions, fostering a social environment through various events and online platforms. With the post-pandemic shift to a hybrid work process, the company has realised the evolving nature of professional relationships, especially for new employees and the younger generation. While in-person connectivity is ideal, the company understands that a balance must be found not to end up in burnout in this era of digitalisation. Thus, achieving equilibrium in a hybrid work setting seems to be the only recipe for the future of work, where OSC creation can move forward and generate added value, to both the organisations' human resource and culture, as well.

Consequently, our findings also point to the delicate interdependence structure in the organisation, where cooperation and teamwork are essential in technological projects. DATA-CO actively encourages team independence, acknowledging their pivotal role in development activities and customer-oriented projects. The flexibility of interdependence types, such as pooled, sequential and reciprocal, is a reflection of the company's flexible and adaptable nature. In summary, the organisational culture of DATA-CO encompasses a dynamic and empowering work environment that maximises employee options for a hybrid work model.

In answering the second research question, namely *What novel influencing factors of OSC are emerging in the mindset of IT&C professionals?*, the exploration of organisational (in)stability and (dis)continuity within DATA-CO in Romania reveals a nuanced understanding of the factors shaping the work environment. Employees acknowledge the importance of internal changes, both locally and worldwide, and recognise the possible impact of high-level politics on stability. The need for adaptivity to new, uncertain futures is emphasised, underlining the organisation landscape as dynamic. Thus, the already established influencing factors of OSC creation (see Nahapiet & Ghoshal, 1998), overlapped with "remote" work arrangements and high fluctuations, typically for the international IT&C setting, generate a more complicated and tangled woven, which asks for embracing novel paradigms such as: *a profile of a virtual leader* or *a virtual organisational culture*.

The study highlights the critical role of communication and transparency in mitigating or exacerbating discontinuities. Effective communication channels, especially in larger teams, prove vital for maintaining stability amid frequent transitions. The findings also reveal the importance of organisational agility to respond to team fluctuations and adapt to evolving technological innovations.

Client perceptions emphasise the company's responsive mechanism to internal concerns and client escalations, classifying disruptions as inputs rather than long-term issues. Although there are high fluctuations rates in the IT&C sector, the analysed company shows resilience in retaining clients and projects, highlighting its ability to manage uncertainties effectively. Therefore, the results indicate the importance of proactive communication, adaptability and transparency in the development of a cohesive and resilient organisational culture in DATA-CO. Nonetheless, the company uses some strategies in order to adapt to changes, such as efficient work distribution, maintaining stability during challenging times and cultivating a collaborative and cohesive spirit among employees.

Our exploration of key influencing factors at DATA-CO, including closure, self-differentiation and the shift to hybrid and remote work, paints a nuanced picture of the organisation's dynamics. The prolonged tenure of employees is revealed to be an important contributor to a strong emotional bond and sense of belonging, playing a crucial role in mitigating attrition. The shift towards transactional relationships, self-identification as a DATA-CO employee and the differentiation from colleagues further illustrate the intricate elements influencing employee satisfaction and retention.

The embrace of hybrid and remote work brings forth varied perspectives. While some view it as a positive change, attributing freshness to social interactions and a positive impact on organisational dynamics, others emphasise individual agency in managing the personal and social aspects of remote work. The capacity to balance in-person and remote work is regarded as essential, requiring further empirical investigation for a comprehensive understanding. Task-related conversations, team dynamics, team dynamics and their effects on management are closely connected to the broader theme of adjusting to flexible work arrangements.

In essence, the happiness of employees at DATA-CO hinges on a delicate interplay of factors. Prolonged tenure fosters a robust emotional bond and a sense of belonging, countering attrition. The organisation's ability to balance transactional relationships provides flexibility for self-expression and creativity, promotes a strong connection with clients and contributes significantly to job satisfaction. Moreover, the company's strategic focus on hybrid and remote work options corresponds with the evolving preferences of employees. The positive impact is evident in perceptions of work-life balance, individual agency in managing professional and personal aspects, and the organisation's competitive advantage in attracting and retaining talent.

Employee contentment at DATA-CO is not merely a product of isolated initiatives but is deeply rooted in the organisational culture. Resilience, adaptability and shared accountability throughout personnel transitions underscore a cohesive team spirit.

Recognition for individual contributions, a supportive management style and the ability to easily reallocate tasks and projects are characteristics of an environment that believes their employees have value and worth. Overall, the key to DATA-CO's workplace culture is its holistic approach that encompasses both personal and professional facets, allowing employees to find fulfilment and satisfaction in their roles.

The qualitative analysis of organisational structure, employee experience and process analysis in DATA-CO confirms the validity of the research's main direction on the characteristics of social capital in a hybrid entrepreneurial environment. The study emphasises an organisation's flexibility to promote trust, cooperation and collaboration in a hybrid business environment by strengthening important social connections through regular meetings and online forms. Evidence of longer-term employee retention, interdependence of groups and early adoption of communication strategies, they all lend credibility to this certification and show how dynamic and durable social capital is in this situation.

REFERENCES

Luthans, F., Luthans, K., Luthans, B., & Peterson, S. (2024). Psychological, physical, and social capitals: A balanced approach for more effective human capital in today's organizations and life. *Organizational Dynamics, 53*(4), 101080. https://doi.org/10.1016/j.orgdyn.2024.101080

Mahajan, R., Lim, W. M., Sareen, M., Kumar, S., & Panwar, R. (2023). Stakeholder theory. *Journal of Business Research, 166*, 114104.

Mishra, N., & Bharti, T. (2024). Exploring the nexus of social support, work–life balance and life satisfaction in hybrid work scenario in learning organizations. *The Learning Organization, 31*(1), 27–47. https://doi.org/10.1108/TLO-08-2022-0099

Nahapiet, J., & Ghoshal, S. (1998). Social capital, intellectual capital, and the organisational advantage. *The Academy of Management Review, 23*(2), 242–266.

Yadav, R., Yadav, M., & Vihari, N. S. (2024). High-performance work system and learning orientation in offline, online, and hybrid workplaces: the mediating role of affective commitment. *The Learning Organization, 31*(1), 122–136. https://doi.org/10.1108/TLO-10-2022-0118

Appendix 1 Interview Question Matrix

Themes	Main questions	Sub-questions and explanation
The 4 original factors influencing the creation of Organisational Social Capital (OSC)		
Interaction	Q1. How would you describe the quantity and quality of social interaction within your organisation at this moment?	Forms of interaction: 1. In-person at the office 2. Hybrid (in-person and remote) 3. Remote from home office

(continued)

(continued)

Themes	Main questions	Sub-questions and explanation
Interdependence	Q2. How do you see the level of interdependence between colleagues at your organisation at this moment?	Types of interdependence: 1. Functional interdependence (e.g. project tasks, daily tasks) 2. Relational interdependence (goes beyond project tasks to include the quality of social relations) 3. Pooled interdependence (teams contribute separately to the organisation but may not directly interact with and depend on other teams) 4. Sequential interdependence (one team produces an output which then acts as an input required for the work/output of another team in the organisation) 5. Reciprocal interdependence (in addition to the sequential one, it is cyclical, reciprocal, the output of a team becomes the input of another whose output then becomes the input of the first team and so forth)
Stability/continuity	Q3. Being aware of the changes in personnel in the labour market overall, how would you characterise the (in)stability/(dis)continuity in personnel within your organisation at this moment?	(In)stability/(dis)continuity in: 1. Social/people structures overall 2. Management team 3. Functional/departmental teams (e.g. HR, Finance, etc.) 4. Project teams (including juniors who may not be directly involved in the project)
Closure	Q4. How would you characterise closure within your organisation at this moment?	Closure is the 4th original factor influencing OSC and refers to: The existence of boundaries that separate those who work at your organisation from other employees not working there, creating a sense of pride and belonging to the organisation ("us" versus "them", e.g. I'm at X, I'm a global digital innovator working for Y, I belong to this organisation and I'm proud of it).
Our 2 additional factors influencing the flow and stock of OSC		

(continued)

APPENDIX 1 INTERVIEW QUESTION MATRIX 87

(continued)

Themes	Main questions	Sub-questions and explanation
Hybrid/remote work	Q5. How would you assess the impact of hybrid and remote work on social interaction within your organisation at this moment?	See Q1 for forms of social interaction in the workplace
	Q6. How would you assess the impact of hybrid and remote work on interdependence within your organisation at this moment?	See Q2 for types of interdependence
Changes in personnel/turnover	Q7. Being aware of the frequent changes in personnel in the labour market overall, how would you assess the impact of the frequent changes in personnel (high turnover) on the stability/continuity of social (people) structures within your organisation at this moment?	See Q3 for info on (in)stability/(dis)continuity in personnel structures
	Q8. How do you see the impact of the frequent changes in personnel (high turnover) on closure within your organisation at this moment?	See Q4 for the definition of closure
Organisational-level constructs of OSC		
Shared identity	Q9. How would you assess the existence of a shared organisational identity at your organisation at this moment?	A shared identity within the organisation refers to a sense of working together for the same organisation to reach common goals
Collective action	Q10. How would you assess the existence of collective action within your organisation now?	Collective action refers to the ability of organisational members (managers, colleagues) to act collectively for common goals (doing things together for a common purpose)
Individual-level constructs of OSC		
Associability	Q11. How would you assess associability within your organisation now?	Associability refers to a focus of the organisational members (managers, colleagues) on joint, common interests instead of individual interests, i.e. the willingness to prioritise collective instead of personal interests and goals

(continued)

(continued)

Themes	Main questions	Sub-questions and explanation
Trust	Q12. How would you characterise the existence of trust between people (be they managers or colleagues) within your organisation now? Q13. How would you characterise the existence of trust in your organisation as a whole now? Q14. What type(s) of trust in managers/colleagues is/are most prevalent within your organisation now? Q15. What type(s) of trust in your organisation as a whole is/are most prevalent now?	Trust refers to a firm belief in the reliability, truth and ability of the organisation and its members (managers, colleagues) Types of trust to assess: 1. Fragile trust: based on rational calculation of risks and rewards, e.g. as in a transaction, occasional, short-term 2. Resilient trust: based on the belief in the moral integrity of colleagues and the organisation, based on repeated interactions over a longer period of time 3. Dyadic trust: between two parties who have direct knowledge of each other 4. Generalised trust: based not on direct knowledge but on affiliation and reputation, and on norms, values and behaviours in the overall organisation
Organisational Social Capital of the future – future scenarios	Q16. How do you see these future possible scenarios concerning building social capital within your organisation? Which scenario is the most and which one is the least plausible and why? Q17. How would you assess the role of these measures in developing social capital within your organisation in future? Q18. How will each of the measures influence Organisational Social Capital?	Future possible scenarios and their impact on Organisational Social Capital: 1. Back to the pre-pandemic situation 2. Continuation of the "work from anywhere" (WFA) model with regular in-person, e.g. once a week, meetings at the organisation 3. Continuation of the WFA model with quarterly 3–4-day workshops in different attractive locations 4. A hybrid model with 2 days in office, 3 days WFA or 3 days in office, 2 days WFA)

(continued)

(continued)

Themes	Main questions	Sub-questions and explanation

		Possible ways to develop Organisational Social Capital in future and reduce the physical and mental distance between the organisation and its employees:
		1. Improving the existing interactive portals between the organisation and its employees as an intermediate step
		2. Developing new interactive portals between the organisation and its employees that provide useful, updated information and support interaction and interdependence as an intermediate step
		3. Adopting and using metaverse as a more advanced possibility, which may facilitate interaction and interdependence at work as well as provide benefits and facilities for spending the free time together with colleagues (including their families/children)
		4. Adding the following features/elements to the existing/new interactive portals:
		  a. Emotional connection elements which can aim to improve managers and colleagues' emotional attachment to the organisation and therefore improve retention within the organisation
		  b. Gamification which can aim to make portals more attractive to use
		  c. Other possible features/elements?
		1. Improving stability/ continuity/ retention in personnel overall within your organisation
		2. Improving stability/ continuity/ retention in project teams within your organisation
		3. Other possible ways?

GPSR Compliance

The European Union's (EU) General Product Safety Regulation (GPSR) is a set of rules that requires consumer products to be safe and our obligations to ensure this.

If you have any concerns about our products, you can contact us on ProductSafety@springernature.com

In case Publisher is established outside the EU, the EU authorized representative is:

Springer Nature Customer Service Center GmbH
Europaplatz 3
69115 Heidelberg, Germany

Batch number: 09253160

Printed by Printforce, the Netherlands